AFRICAN CANADIANS UNDER LEGAL, JUDICIAL, POLITICAL, POLICE AND MEDIA ATTACK

DR. MUNYONZWE HAMALENGWA

GIFT *Certificate*

TO:

FROM:

DATE:

AFRICAN CANADIANS UNDER LEGAL, JUDICIAL, POLITICAL, POLICE AND MEDIA ATTACK

Dr. Munyonzwe Hamalengwa
PhD (Law).

ACP PRESS
www.africaincanadapress.com

TORONTO, CANADA – 2017

African Canadians under Legal, Judicial, Political, Police and Media Attack

PUBLISHED BY:

AFRICA IN CANADA PRESS
18A-100 Westmore Drive, Toronto, ON M9V 5C3, CANADA
Tel: 1 (416) 644-1106, Fax: 1 (416) 644-1126
http://www.africaincanadapress.com

AFRICA IN CANADA PRESS is committed to publishing works by authors of African descent in Canada and abroad with excellence.

BOOK DESIGNED AND DEVELOPED BY:

DIAMOND BOOKS
www.diamondbooks.ca

PAPERBACK EDITION - ISBN: 978-1-988251-05-9 – AFRICA IN CANADA PRESS
E-BOOK EDITION - ISBN: 978-1-988357-45-4 – DIAMOND PUBLISHERS

PRINTED IN CANADA

DEDICATION

Dudley Laws and **Charles Roach**, true heroes of the African Canadian struggles in Canada in the second half of the 20th Century and first decade of the 21st Century.

ACKNOWLEDGEMENT

In the Fall of 1994, a group of African-Canadians met at the Ontario Institute for Studies in Education (OISIE) to plot and counter attack against the racial profiling, racism and discrimination that the community was subjected to. Some of those in attendance have since left us: **Dudley Laws**, **Charles Roach**, **Bev Folkes** and others. I wish to acknowledge and thank all those in attendance, for that meeting was the Genesis of this book. Racial profiling, racism and discrimination continue in Ontario, Canada and the USA, unabated, hence the need for this book.

I praise **Dr. Ajamu Nangwaya** for his permission to reproduce his compilation of African-Canadian victims of police brutality. The evidence is overwhelming.

I wish to thank most profusely, **Diamond Books - Canada** for typesetting the manuscript in perfect form that is pleasing to the eye. I wish to thank **Diamond Publishers** for bringing out this book in record time after getting the manuscript.

At the end of the day, I am solely responsible for what appears in this book that I have personally said or written. Others are responsible for what they said or wrote.

Dr. Munyonzwe Hamalengwa
Dean, School of Law
The Zambian Open University, Lusaka,

March 13, 2017

TABLE OF CONTENTS

CHAPTERS

CHAPTER 1

INTRODUCTION

Over the last decade or so the Toronto media, particularly the *Toronto Star* and community media like *Share* and *Pride* newspapers and the *Caribbean Camera* has reported on study after new studies relating to racial discrimination or racism perpetrated against African Canadians by persons, agencies and institutions that are central to the supposed equal application and benefit of the law pursuant to section 15 of the Charter and related sections of the Ontario Human Rights Code, without discrimination on the basis of race and other grounds. The racial discrimination and racism perpetrated by the practices of these law administration and enforcement persons, agencies and institutions violate also sections 8, 9 and 27 of the Charter and related sections of the Ontario Human Rights Code.

These studies were reported by the media in total isolation from each other but they are entirely connected and we must insist on the connection of these studies albeit they were done in isolation but their release on occasions is positive.

One study released in November 2015 by the Community Assessment of Police Practices found that the policy of carding that had supposedly been outlawed by the Toronto Police Services Board has actually been ignored by the police on the beat and that carding continues unabated. What is most distressing is that a lot of faith had been placed by the community in that initiative that for once something was being implemented to accord with their political, legal and moral pressure on the Chief of Police and the Toronto Police Services Board to address and redress their grievances. But now to no avail. Other very distressing aspects of the revelation of the continued carding are the responses of the Chair of the Board who while disappointed with the results of the study, deferred to the reaction of the police chief. The Police Chief's reaction was most distressing. Instead of embracing the results of the study and promising to do better in outlawing carding and racial profiling, the Police Chief instead, attacked the study and the luke-warm reaction of the Chair of the Police Services Board.

In other words, the Toronto Police Chief had not yet gotten it, that carding and racial profiling continue to be practiced by his force at the expense of the constitutional rights of African Canadians. This carding and racial profiling is not limited to the youth or to African Canadians driving expensive cars. It catches every African Canadian who is unfortunate to be the target that day.

The continued carding and racial profiling further justifies the continued class action law suits against these practices by the Black Action Defense Committee that were launched beginning in 2013 and beyond against Toronto Police, Durham Police, Peel Police and Federal Correctional Facilities. These suits are in the process of being amended and judges have already been assigned to case manage them. BADC continues to call on those carded and racially profiled and who have documentation to come forward.

The decades-old struggles of African-Canadians and their allies have produced positive results in the recent past in that reform initiatives against carding have been drafted by the Government as represented by the Ministry of Community Safety and Correctional Services in the Fall of 2015 and

the Government of Ontario announced the creation of an Anti-Racism Secretariate in February 2016. The Ministry had previously been sued by BADC although on consent the suit against the Minister was withdrawn but the suit against carding and racial profiling will continue.
It has to be stated that reforming carding practices does not eliminate racial profiling. Racial profiling is a more embedded practice of racial policing and needs systemic routing by way of class action law suits than mere legislation would permit. Racial profiling is permitted by law and the reforms on carding do not address the law respecting racial profiling. One needs only to read cases from the Human Rights Tribunal of Ontario on racial profiling where police officers openly admit to their use of discretion to do almost anything they want under the High Way Traffic Act.

Racial profiling or discrimination is not limited to the police. African-Canadian children are more apprehended by Children's Aid Societies disproportionate to their population than other children. Black children are more expelled or suspended from schools across the province than mandated. Central institutions like the Law Society of Upper Canada released a study in November 2014 which documented that African

Canadian lawyers in Ontario are subjected to endemic racism, racial discrimination, racial profiling, harassment and marginalization within the legal profession.

It is clear therefore that carding which supposedly only affects the youth or African Canadians driving expensive cars is not only mythical, it is an untruth as racism and racial discrimination, racial profiling and harassment practices are broader and more systemic than that. They are perpetrated against African Canadians who are supposed to have made it in the supposedly one of the safest harbours in Canada, the legal profession. And this racism, racial discrimination, racial profiling, harassment and marginalization practices are perpetrated by the men and women of the law in the legal profession and legal institutions. These are people who are supposed to know the constitution, people who swear to uphold the law? It can be seen that carding is not an outlier, it is embedded and finds support within the legal system.

Over twenty years ago, in October (1994), Charles Roach, Dudley Laws, MunyonzweHamalengwa, MigunaMiguna, Norman Otis Richmond, Afua Pam Cooper, Kike Roach, Marlene Norbese Philip, Colin Browne, Bev Folks, Enid Lee and many other community members met at The University of Toronto and denounced racism, racial discrimination, harassment and marginalization perpetrated against African Canadians by the Judiciary, the politicians, the police, the legal profession, the media and mainstream society in general. The third Chapter of this book contains the transcript of that Conference. What has changed over the decades or years? Chapter two is an over-view of police-minority relations in historic perspective. I gave this paper in Sydney, Australia in 1989.

Class action law suits were contemplated because of the unresponsive nature of political, police, judicial and other influences to the plight of African Canadians. This is the subject of Chapter four. Chapter five is a letter representing one of the tools of struggle used among many others to influence action by the powers-that-be.

The practices of racial profiling have occasionally led to shootings of black men and women. The paper by Dr. Ajamu Nangwaya which is Chapter 6 is an itemization of provable encounters between the law enforcement agencies in Canada and African Canadians.

Chapter seven is a generic factum that could be submitted in the application for certification of a class action law suit. Chapter eight is an appeal to the centres of power to do something about the unequal application and benefit of the law pertaining to African Canadians. The provenance of and continuation of racism and racial discrimination against African Canadians, no matter what their supposed station in life is, is no longer anecdotal.

- **Dr. Munyonzwe Hamalengwa**

Sunday, February 28, 2016.
Toronto, CANADA.

CHAPTER 2

A CONTRIBUTION TO THE DEBATE ON CIVILIAN CONTROL OF POLICE POWERS IN TORONTO, 1988.

Dr. Munyonzwe Hamalengwa

A Paper Presented to: Investigating Crime And Apprehending Suspects: Police Powers and Citizens Rights, Conference Organized By The Society For The Reform of the Criminal Law, Sydney, Australia, March 19th-24th, 1989.

It is contended by Michael Valpy of the Globe and Mail, a major Canadian National Newspaper, that the Toronto Police Commission, the Toronto Police Force Commanders and the Toronto Police Union all refuse to acknowledge that there is a rift between the police and so-called "visible minorities". Yet in a recent poll by The Environics

Group, nearly 50 percent of all those polled said the police should be doing a better job in that area as opposed to 37 percent who said the police were doing a good job in that area. On the overall 74 percent of the respondents said the Toronto police was good or excellent.

Environics found that the Ontario police force was composed of 92 percent white males; 5 percent white women; 2.3 percent visible minorities and 0.2 percent were aboriginals.[1] These statistics are a backdrop to the recent strained relations in Toronto between the police force and "visible minorities", mainly black as a result of the police shooting to death of two black men in the Toronto area in 1988. One a disabled man, by the name of Lester Donaldson was shot in his apartment in August and the other, a 17-year old Michael Wade Lawson was shot while driving a stolen car in December. Two police officers were charged, one with manslaughter and other with aggravated assault for the Lawson killing. After six months of investigation one police officer was charged with manslaughter for the Donaldson killing.

These police shootings of blacks are reminiscent of several others that date back to 1978 when a black youth by the name of Buddy Evans was shot by the police. The police shooting to death of Albert

Johnson in 1979 led to a near riot by the blacks in Toronto. These shootings have triggered in the black community in Toronto and in other quarters as well as elsewhere the possible need to have some kind of civilian control over the use of police powers. Are the police a law unto themselves? What could be done?

This paper is a contribution to that debate. It is mainly descriptive and is intended for readers who are not very familiar with the goings-on in Toronto between the police force and visible minorities. It does not claim to be an exhaustive statement on the issue.

Before I proceed, I have to add a caveat here in order to contextualize the issues I will be discussing: the media from which we learn most things that are going on around us including the turmoil between the Toronto police and visible minorities has a tendency to overblow some issues out of proportion to their actual gravity. I am not necessarily saying that the issue of the strained relations between the Toronto police and visible minorities has been overblown, I am suggesting that it is important to bear in mind that some issues are usually overblown by the media. Overblowing some issues is in fact inherent to the operations of the media just as ignoring or underplaying of some issues is also inherent to the media.[2]

Official Response:

In the wake of the incidents mentioned above, the Solicitor-General for Ontario who is in charge of the police, struck a task force to examine police-minority relations and to make recommendations. The task force was named Race Relations and Policing Task Force (RRPTF). This task force started hearings in early February 1989. Several issues are being raised. One of the issues raised when the task force was announced was that there had been four similar studies in the past 10 years which had not brought about any improvements.[3] Legislative moves have also not worked. Another issue debated in the hearings was whether the hiring of more visible minorities into the police force would improve the situation. It was noted that of the 2,000 police officers in Toronto, only 200 were from visible minorities. This obviously did not reflect Toronto's cultural mosaic.4 Some noted that hiring more visible minorities is not the answer because the hired police officers will in due course adopt a police mentality which is structural to the functions of policing. Even if this did not happen it is likely that minority police officers will be coerced into conformity, something that happens all the time. It was also suggested that more education may be the answer. It has also been mentioned that perhaps the police should not carry firearms as this may tempt them to use them unnecessarily. But the dominant opinion seems not to associate violence as emanating from the police. Police are not seen as using violence against the people. For example, in a major study sponsored by The John Howard Society of Canada, a major Canadian think tank, entitled Insights into Violence in Contemporary Canadian Society containing conference papers by prominent Canadian Crimmologists, both legal and sociological, I could only find two references in one paper to the possibility of police violence in the process of investigating violent crimes.[5] The police are regarded as "legitimacy incarnate."[6]

International opinion on the carrying of firearms by law enforcement agencies seems to be more advanced than domestic Canadian attitudes on this issue. Article 3 for example of the United Nations Code of Conduct for Law Enforcement Officials stipulates, "Law enforcement officials may use force only when strictly necessary and to the extent required for the performance of their duty." One of the explanations for this article is that the use of firearms is considered an extreme measure and that every effort should be made to exclude the use of firearms especially against children. Firearms should not be used except when a suspected offender offers resistance or jeopardizes the lives of others.

These observations culled from international opinion are pertinent in the Canadian context. Albert Johnson in 1979 and Lester Donaldson in 1988 were both shot in their houses allegedly unarmed. Anthony Griffin, a black youth shot in Montreal in 1987 and Michael Wade Lawson, another black youth killed in Toronto in 1988 were both shot in the back, indicating they probably were running away and not posing any immediate danger to the police or to others. In all these cases and others, the use of the firearm was critical. Couldn't other methods have been used to effect the arrests?

Section 25(3) of the Criminal Code[7] of Canada permits in criminal enforcement the use of as much force as is possible -- even that which leads to death to protect police officers or others. The Supreme Court of Canada has recently ruled that the safety of police officers or third parties can justify the use of force by the police. But the police must have grounds to believe a real threat of violence exists.[8] However, force here should not be read to mean "to shoot to kill." Force is used in the context of executing a search warrant. But it is clear from the Criminal Code that if force leads to death or serious bodily harm, so long it was applied in order to preserve the lives of police officers or others it is justifiable. Uncalled for excessive force would attract criminal sanctions provided for in Sec. 26 of the Criminal Code. The difficult part is to determine or judge whether police officers can gauge correctly that the suspect or criminal is about to apply lethal force against them or others. Is uncontrolled force used easily when the police are pursuing a member of the visible minority? Members of the visible minority say this seems on the evidence to be the case.

Another position which is strongly supported by Alan Borovoy, the General Counsel to the Canadian Civil Liberties Association is to institute across the Province of Ontario civilian bodies that will oversee police conduct and practices.[9] A modified civilian body already exists in Toronto. It has not been effective.

The rest of this paper discusses in summary form the history and politics of the plea of creating civilian bodies in Ontario to oversee police behaviour. I will conclude with my own suggestions.

Civilian Bodies and the Police:
In this paper I am mainly concerned with civilian control or review of police powers in regard to police-visible minority relations. By civilian control or review of police powers I restrict to mean civilian run investigations and adjudications of alleged police misconduct. This means these roles are taken away from police forces. However the concern over police powers is broader than this: it encompasses control of police discretion, independent review of complaints against police, entrapment, exclusion of illegally-obtained evidence, civil and criminal proceedings and abuse of process.[10] As already stated I will not concern myself with some of these broader issues except with that of independent review of complaints against the police.

A brief wider review is in order here. The broader context that attracted public outcry for civilian control of police powers has to be traced to the early seventies when massive wrongdoings by police forces, especially the Royal Canadian Mounted Police (RCMP) were uncovered. This in turn can be traced to the political crisis originating in Quebec. The RCMP wrongdoings led to major commissions, investigations, the most well-known being the McDonald Commission of Inquiry Concerning Certain Activities of the

R.C.M.P.[11] It was found that the RCMP had engaged in illegal activities which included break-ins, arson, buggings, theft of mail and documents, etc.[12] The concern was that the police had become a law unto themselves with no accountability and without any effective independent control.
Hitherto the practice was that if there were any allegations against the police, the police would investigate themselves and would impose any sanctions internally. (This is still largely the case). This obviously was a suspicious practice from the point of view of those who suffered transgressions as police would likely protect their personnel from external forces. The Report of the Commission of Inquiry Relating to Public Complaints, Internal Discipline and Grievance Procedure within the R.C.M.P. (1976) - The Marin Report did indeed sanction the status quo. It "favoured the retention of all stages of the investigation and adjudication within police hands but with the imposition of a Federal Police Ombudsman to oversee the system and ensure that justice was done to both the citizen and the police concerned."[13] This was not accepted or followed.

An Ontario Provincial report, The Royal Commission Report into Metropolitan Police Practices (1976) - The Morand Report "favoured a system which would place more of the important decisions in hands not connected with the police."[14] This was not followed either. A modified version is in place.

Professor Alan Grant of Osgoode Hall Law School posits 5 possible models for handling citizen-police complaints.[15] The models are: (1) The "in-house" one, which entails that "the duty to record the complaint, to investigate and adjudicate upon it would be in the hands of the police."[16] (2) The externally supervised "in-house" model. This model ensures that "the investigation and adjudication functions follow the "in-house" model but there is an external review factor built in at the end of the process."[17] (3) The police investigation with independent adjudication model. This is where the "investigation of complaints would...be conducted by the police, but once the investigation was completed, the adjudication and disposition would be in the hands of a body independent of the police."[18] (4) The independent investigation with police adjudication model. In this model, the investigation would not be in the hands of the police but would be conducted by investigators employed specifically for the purpose and make recommendations to the chief of police who would dispose of the case. (5) The last model Grant calls the "truly independent" model, where all facets of the complaint, from it initially being recorded until disposition, would be kept out of police hands entirely. This is the model I support.

Ontario has more of the "in-house" model i.e. the first model whereby investigation and adjudication is entirely in the hands of the police. Visible minorities distrust this model because they believe it white-washes police wrongdoing.

The shootings of members of visible minorities are obviously regarded as police wrongdoings. Because the police investigate themselves, most times except when there is public outcry, no charges are laid against alleged offending police officers. According to Edward Greenspan, a prominent Canadian Criminal lawyer, the shooting to death of Albert Johnson in 1979 was the first time in the history of Metropolitan Toronto police force that a charge of manslaughter was laid against an officer.[19] It took six months to have a charge laid against the officer who shot Lester Donaldson. Why did it take such a long time to lay these charges? So far also, all police officers who are charged end up being acquitted. Are the courts also in on this?

The shooting to death of Albert Johnson in 1979 triggered a mass movement to make the police accountable.[20] The police raid on Toronto gay bathhouses only fuelled the momentum for civilian review and control of police powers. Groups such as Working Group on Minority-Police Relations were formed. A more well-known group formed was a group called Citizen's Independent Review of Police Activities (CIRPA) which was formed in 1981. The aims of CIRPA were:

1. To systematically obtain and review allegations of police misconduct in Metropolitan Toronto.

2. To assist complainants in pursuing their allegations through the most appropriate channels.

3. To publish periodically statistics on the number and nature of complaints and on their disposition and also on counter-charges laid by the police. These statistics should include divisions, names and numbers of police officers.

4. To press for reforms to ensure that both complainants and police officers receive fair and impartial treatment.

5. To conduct research into and to press for needed reforms in the organization and conduct of the Metropolitan Toronto Police Force.

6. To give information to other sympathetic groups and individuals (e.g. lawyers) approved by the board of directors.

7. To be concerned with public education.

8. To initiate legal and other actions which are consistent with the goals of the organization as well as intervening in and sponsoring litigation.

CIRPA was criticized for being no more than a "pressure group of the farleft" "of like-minded individuals, who had no patience with the views or interests of the larger public."[22] But as McMahon and Ericson report, this citizen's group ended up by being incorporated into the States' Agenda, with very little teeth.[23] The state was also busy at the same putting out reform packages to meet the crises and citizen's concerns. Some of the initiatives included the enacting of The Metropolitan Police Force Complaints Project Act, 1981, which set up the office of the Public Complaints Commissioner among other reforms.

This Act was repealed in 1984 by the Metropolitan Toronto Police Force Complaints Act, 1984. Essentially the office of the Public Complaints Commissioner was to create a parallel complaints system against the police. Previously a person had to complain only to the police force. A person can now complain either through the Police Complaints Forum or the Public Complaints Commissioner. The major problem with the office of the Public Complaints Commissioner is that the investigation and adjudication is still in the hands of the police. The CIRPA has no independent power so it works through the Police Commission, the Public Complaints Commissioner and legal channels. It may as well not be existing. According to McMahon and Ericson the CIRPA has been overtaken by the "middle-class" types--lawyers etc. who may not be closer to the people who are at the receiving end of police misconduct.[24]

But at the end of the day any complaint by the public against a police officer would likely end up in one of four ways: dismissal of complaint; internal discipline of the officer involved; civil action against the concerned officer or criminal proceedings. Internal discipline is hard to monitor, given that even officers who are criminally charged and are in the public eye continue to work and be paid. All these methods of police control focus on the individual officer and not the police force. They thus do not lead to structural reform. All police officers who have been charged for shooting minorities have been acquitted. This may mean that even civil proceedings may not be successful. However, one of the major possible effects of civil and criminal proceedings is general deterrence against police abuse. Lack of convictions however will continue to cause concerns.

Lack of convictions may be because of the manner in which complaints are investigated and adjudicated--by the police themselves. It may be that the most effective system would be model 5 discussed above of citizen-police complaints system whereby initial investigation through to adjudication is out of police hands. This would be done by an independent body. This model is not likely to be accepted but in the final analysis it seems to me to be the best model to reduce tensions between the police and visible minorities. The police and the state have nothing to fear from the model as the judicial system will sort out impartially the baseless from the credible complaints.

The creation of a Race Relations and Policing Task Force by the Ontario Solicitor General on December 15, 1988 is a good beginning.
Its terms of reference are limited to the following:

1. The current training members of police forces receive as it relates to visible minorities.

2. Ways to improve this training and education both for recruits and on a continuing education basis.

3. The hiring practices and promotional processes including the establishment of employment equity programs.
4. Ways to improve the interaction of the police with the visible minority communities through the establishment of liaison officers, committees, community education programs and cross cultural training.

5. To examine ways in which a monitoring system may be established to provide for a regular review of the interaction between visible minorities and the police.

6. To review the policies and practices of the police relating to the use of force.

Given the numerous studies already undertaken, it is hoped that this will move the ground a little bit forward. I am in agreement with Robert Peel when he stated the following a long time ago:

"The test of police efficiency is the absence of crime and disorder, not the visible evidence of police action in dealing with them."

"The ability of the police to perform their duties is dependent upon public approval of police existence, actions, behaviour, and the ability of the police to secure and maintain public respect".25

NOTE:
Chapters 6 and 8 update this chapter.

END NOTES

1. The statistics in the first and this portion of the paragraph are summarized in Michael Valpy, "Problem Will Stay Until it is Admitted" Toronto *Globe and Mail* 24 January, 1989, p. A8. It is not only the police force that does not hire visible minorities, rather this trend is endemic in both the governmental institutions and the corporate world, see, Leslie Papp, "Minorities Excluded From Corporate Elite" *Toronto Star*, 5 February, 1989, p. B4.

2. On media "over-coverage of" violence during the commission of a crime, See Anthony Doob, "Portrayals of Violence in the Mass Media" in *Insights Into Violence in Contemporary Canadian Society* edited by James M. Maclatchie (Ottawa: The John Howard Society of Canada, 1987) pp. 57-64.

3. Timothy Appleby and Donn Downey, "Fear of Police has Ruined System" *Globe and Mail*, 2 February, 1989, p. A1.

4. Ibid.

5. Alan Grant, "Emerging Trends in Law Enforcement/Policing" in the above mentioned study edited by James M. Maclatchie, *supra,* note 2, pp. 355-360 at pp. 355 and 359.

6. Maeve McMahon and Richard Ericson, "Reforming the Police and Policing Reform" in *State Control: Criminal Justice Politics in Canada,* edited by R.S. Ratner and John L. McMullan (Vancouver: UBC Press, 1987) p. 38.

7. R.S.C. 1985 c. (46)

8. *Genest v.* R, *Lawyers Weekly*, 10 February, 1989, p. 8 (not yet reported).

9. Timothy Appleby, "Minorities Rejected by Police" *Globe and Mail*, 4 February, 1989, p. A6.

10. See, Alan Grant, Intensive Programme in Criminal Law, Osgoode Hall Law School, Winter 1988, Chapter 3.57.

11. (Ottawa: Minister of Supply and Services, 1979).

12. See Ibid, and *Globe and Mail*, 5 June, 1978.

13. Grant, supra note 10, Chapter 3.81.

14. Ibid.

15. Alan Grant, "The Control of Police Behaviour" in Walter Tarnopolsky (ed.) Some Civil Liberties Issues of the Seventies (Toronto: Carswell, 1975) pp. 74-111, excerpted in Grant, Ibid at 3.103.

16. Ibid.

17. Ibid.

18. Ibid.

19. Edward L. Greenspan and George Jonas, *Greenspan: The Case for the Defence* (Toronto: MacMillan, 1987), p. 177.

20. Ibid p. 178. For a fuller study, see M. McMahon and R. V. Ericson, *Policing Reform: A Study of the Reform Process and Police Institution in Toronto* (Toronto: Centre of Criminology, University of Toronto, 1984).

21. In *supra,* note 6, p. 42.

22. Greenspan, supra, note 19, p. 183.

23. *Supra*, note 6.

24. *Supra,* note 6, p. 43.

25. Sir Robert Peel, 1829 (founder of the modern police force in England) cited in *Policing in Ontario for the Eighties: Perceptions and Reflections,* Report of the Task Force On the Racial and Ethnic Implications of Police Hiring, Training, Promotion and Career Development July 1980. Submitted to the Honourable Roy McMurtry, Solicitor General, p. 37-38.

CHAPTER 3

AFRICAN-CANADIANS UNDER LEGAL, JUDICIAL, POLITICAL, POLICE AND MEDIA ATTACK (1994)

Dr. Munyonzwe Hamalengwa

Today's topic is "African-Canadians under Judicial, political, police and Media Attack: Strategies for Survival". The speakers are lined up in front of you. To my left is Marlene Norbese Philip. She has worked for the community for several years. She has written extensively. Three of her books are outside. If you have some time you can peruse through them. More importantly, if you have money, you can buy them. To my immediate right is Afua Pam Cooper, who has been doing excellent work also in the community for many, many years. She is a poet, academic, rabble rouser, activist, everything. Back to Marlene. I don't need to mention anything about

Marlene in that regard. You know her record. That's why I didn't introduce her in that light. She is a lawyer, if you want to know anything more about that.

Kike Roach, whom I didn't know actually for many years until relatively recently, and I still need some explanation as to why I didn't know her, is seated next to Afua. She is the daughter of Charles Roach, who is at my extreme left.

Kike Roach, from what I have learned of her in the recent past, has been around also doing excellent work in the community. And when she speaks later on you will know what I am talking about.

Charles Roach doesn't need any introduction whatsoever. I will leave it at that.

My name is Munyonzwe Hamalengwa, I am a lawyer and ... also My book is outside as well.

Afua Cooper has just come out with a book, by the way, that is also outside, that is on Canadian Black history. Charles Roach is a poet. Have you brought your book, Collection of Poems.

MR. CHARLES ROACH: No. I have two books, actually.

MUNYONZWE HAMALENGWA: After I have made my remarks, Marlene Norbese Philip will speak, then Afua Cooper, then Kike Roach, then Charles Roach. We will take some questions after that. Then in the afternoon Miguna will be sitting where I am sitting right now. Miguna Miguna is a lawyer and an author. Two of his books are outside there. Both of them have come out in the recent past, two months ago in fact. Once you hear Miguna speak you know he will be around with us for a long time doing excellent work.
In the afternoon also there will be Normal Otis Richmond, who is a broadcaster, community activist, and who has been around also for many, many years doing excellent work in the community. Dudley Laws will also be here in the afternoon. Dudley Laws needs no introduction. And Colin Browne, a lawyer and community activist will also be speaking in the afternoon.

For a long time I was puzzled as to why the mainstream media were making allegations that the Black community commit disproportionately more criminal offenses than other people.

It was only until relatively recently that I discovered why that was so. The reason is that Blacks are under strict scrutiny under the law than any other group. If you are overly scrutinized under the law you are more likely to be arrested, detained, taken to court, sentenced, and hopefully paroled or deported. And if you are under the strictest surveillance of the law you are at the brunt and the receiving end of the criminal justice system. Whereas, others who are not under the bull's eyes of the law are obviously not likely to be at the brunt and receiving end of the criminal justice system. Why? The reason is simple. Because they are above the horizon of the law. As simple as all that. They are above the radar screen of the law. So if you want to escape the criminal justice system, you have to make yourself, bring yourself to the ambit of being above the law. Even my four-month old daughter, under examination in-chief will tell you that if you are under the law you are at the brunt of the criminal justice system. You have to bring yourself above the law. You don't even need to cross-examine her to get that kind of information.

Today's topic is Blacks, or rather "African-Canadians Under Legal , Judicial, Police and Media Attack". Most of the speakers, if not all the speakers, will be examining either general issues on this topic or specific issues. My remarks will be limited to giving examples of how Blacks had been under attack in the political system, under the legal system, police, judiciary and media. These examples are not exhaustive. Others will give more far-reaching examples than I can. And I will leave some of the specific examples to them. And we hope that each speaker will propose at the end of the day or at the end of their speeches, concrete plans of action, what we should do to ameliorate the increasing attacks, what we should do to respond to these attacks.

It is my thesis that African-Canadians have been under increasing attacks in the political system, in the law by the police, by the media. This thing is not new. It has always been the case. But in the recent past the attacks have been more virulent, consistent, deep and broad. There is some pathological reaction going out there in the mainstream society against the African-Canadians. The recent attacks are frightening because of their frequency, consistency and their virulence.

The prior attacks were at least not as broad or deep as the current attacks.

In the political arena we didn't have mayors openly attacking African-Canadians like June Rowlands did not long ago when she said that Black youth committed disproportionately more crimes. We didn't have the leader of the Liberal Party in Ontario openly saying that African-Canadians, specifically Somalians, are involved in welfare frauds. We didn't have a federal party like the Reform Party, whose raison de tre is basically because of its anti-immigrant stand. We didn't have an immigration critic at the federal level whose popularity is dependent on his attacking immigrants.

The Reform Party nearly became the opposition party. Can you imagine that? We nearly had an opposition party that is openly racist. That's new in Canada.

You had a prominent member of the Progressive Conservative Party of Canada, John Crosbie, openly attacking African-Canadians and women. That was not the case in the far past.

In the near future you will have a mayor of Toronto, June Rowland, who will be supported by a police chief who may be Julian Fantino, who you know very well. That is a formidable combination.

And I will talk more about attacks on Blacks by police in a while. But these are just a few examples at the political level.

Regarding the law, a judge recently said -- and I quote, it is in my book -- responding to criticisms by African-Canadians when a police officer was acquitted in a shooting incident. The judge said:

"The officer who fired the shot is extremely fortunate that the accused did not get shot. If that had happened, no doubt, irresponsible members of the legal profession would have demanded murder charges be made."

He went on to say:

“Accompanied by such irresponsible statements such as: ”Black people are sick of being shot by police."

This is a judge now talking. Even judges are beginning to attack African-Canadians. It was not like this in the far past.
A judge also recently stated the following:
"Canada does not deserve such a thug."

Judges are beginning to use the street language, violent street language. They are pandering to the media. The media and judges are in fact competing as to who can make the most violent statements that are catchy and that will be reported by the press. And that's frightening. It never used to be like that.

You now have groups of individuals going to courts when someone is going to be sentenced to impress on the judges to give those guys longer sentences. That never used to be the case. There used to be victim impact statements. Now groups are actually going to the courts to impress on the judges to give longer sentences. And the judges are beginning to pander to that.

There are four recently reported cases where this group had gone to court. Two individuals got longer sentences than the normal range, and because of that group. And it's not surprising that at the end of the day people who will be the victims of these groups will be African-Canadians. There is absolutely no doubt about that. The representatives of these groups are white Canadians, and the judges accepting the recommendations of these groups are also white Canadians.

You now have police officers attending immigration and parole hearings to tell the adjudicators not to release specific individuals, and the adjudicators and judges are beginning to pander to that. That's very frightening.

The Chief Justice of Canada, at the last Canadian Bar Association Conference out West, raised the fears about the possible subversion of the administration of justice as a result of media coverage and pressure. He does not need to go very far. The judges are already cow-towing, increasingly so, to the media pressure. And the victims are always, in my submission, the African-Canadians.

We also have lawyers quoted by the media openly stating that the low turn out at the recent Ontario Commission on Systemic Racism in the Ontario Criminal Justice System is attributable to the fact that there is no racism in Ontario. And this was the chairperson of the Criminal Lawyers' Association being quoted as saying such things. They would not even interview Charles Roach; they would not even interview Marlene Norbese or other lawyers who are more connected to those issues. They seek out mainstream lawyers. So not only are judges attacking African-Canadians, even prominent lawyers are attacking African-Canadians.

You go to court as an African-Canadian lawyer -- and most of you have your own experiences in your own field. My experience is that last week when I ordered a transcript of a trial I did, I found out that anytime I was making submissions the judge would say "Mr. Hamalengwa is making assertions." Whereas, whenever she referred to the crown she would say the crown is "taking the position." I was making assertions, the crown is taking a position. There is a difference here.

One judge, in a case that was quite long and very, should we say, controversial, was whenever the crown attorney lost a motion he would preface his remarks by saying, "despite your able arguments" Mr. so and so and so, and he would mention the name of the crown, "I have to decline your motion". Whenever my motion was dismissed, the judge would just say "motion dismissed", and looking somewhere else with contempt in his voice. And, you know, clients can observe this. The language between the crown attorney and the judge is frightening. They look, they conspire. We see this. And it's part of the game in these courtrooms. And there are numerous examples. In fact, each one of you have your own examples from your own practices.

The police. Julian Fantino may be the next police chief. You know what he did when he was stationed in the Jane-Finch area. He started compiling a secret file on African-Canadians who are perceived to be a threat. You can't even be allowed to exercise your own democratic rights in this country. Today I read in the paper that even Susan Eng has had a secret intelligence report on her, someone who is the head of the Police Services Board. I also read in the papers today that there is a secret intelligence report on Somalis in Canada. Who knows how many of you are on that list. My friend Charles is already on that secret list. And you don't know how many other lists he is on. You can't even be allowed to exercise democratic rights in this country.

Art Lymer is constantly attacking African-Canadians. As a matter of fact, as late as August 8th, 1994, there is a report in the *Toronto Star* about his recent remarks regarding Blacks. It's constant.

Whenever I go to court involving a Nigerian, police officers come to me and say, you should come to the police station and see the files we have on these Nigerian welfare scammers, and the insurance fraudsters. So they allege that Nigerians are involved in these things. Yet, all reports indicate that everybody out there in the community, some of them are on welfare because of economic crisis, but they single out Somalis and Nigerians as being on welfare or scamming the welfare system.

Kike Roach is going to talk about the numerous Blacks who are shot by the police. But that is an aspect of the attacks that we have been suffering from over the years.

Regarding the media, you know our friend Christie Blatchford of the Toronto Sun. Her raison detre is to hunt niggers. That's all she does. She has a radio show. Most of the topics discussed there involve “niggers”. Recently she stated that in reporting on a case where some people filed a complaint about a police officer, she asked the following question:
"The more interesting I think is why they come to Canada where the presumption of prejudice is nourished."

Before that she said:
"Where do they come from, these sad, obsessed people, Budria, Shaheedmian, Lesley McLean."

There is one African-Canadian and two are of East-Asian orientation. So you can't even be allowed to feel that this is your country. They constantly ask you where you come from. You may even have been born here.

The other day she attacked Arnold Minors. Here is the newspaper cutting. It was because he associated with Dudley Laws. They don't even know that their view of criminal convictions is different from our view of criminal convictions. Arnold Minors should not associate with Dudley Laws, a member of our community, yet they are associating with people like Mario Gentile who has been convicted. The other day when he announced his resignation a lot of people went to his side, a lot of people, mainstream people. They don't even call him a convicted criminal at all. But we should not associate with our own people regardless of how much they have done for the community. And you have no forum to respond to the attacks. And I will come to that.

They write everyday about our problems. But we have absolutely no forum whereby we could respond to these attacks. We should have a forum where we should respond to these attacks.

The *Toronto Sun* used to be a peripheral tabloid. It's no longer a peripheral tabloid. It's a mainstream tabloid. It's the largest circulating paper on Sundays. And you know many people read papers on Sundays because they don't do much except read papers. The Toronto Sun is the largest circulating paper. And in the recent past there was a good article in the *Now Magazine* which indicated that the Toronto Sun is actually moving into mainstream, it's out there, and that more people read it now than ever before. The *Globe & Mail*, believe you me, maybe sidelined in the near future.

The *Toronto Star*, people disdain it because of its unprincipled liberalism. You don't know whether they are coming or going. Even some of the good reporters, that I regard as good reporters like Rosie Di Mano sometimes you are so happy with her article, and then sometimes you say, My God, what's wrong with this woman. One article is very good. But next to it she will write something outrageous. You have no forum where you can be consistent. We need to create a forum where we can be consistent.

The media now attend immigration and parole hearings, to make it known to adjudicators that they are there to report. And when the adjudicators see the media they will pander to the media. That is an aspect where we are under attack. They will more likely attend hearings involving African-Canadians than other people.

The Logan Brothers, is one of the most notorious examples of what I am talking about in terms of how Blacks are under attach, precisely because a day before his parole hearing, the Scales of Justice program aired on CBC his criminal case. Obviously, it was not surprising that it (parole) was denied, because everybody knew what that man had done.

One time, on the very day I was going to defend -- to assist someone at a deportation hearing in Kingston, the *Toronto Sun* published an article with the picture of the woman in the *Toronto Sun*. I think the title was "Torturer Wants Her Children Back", the very day I was trying to help her to beat the deportation. It is not surprising that they denied that woman the right to come out. She had very good grounds for coming out. Thus, we are under attack on many fronts and we need to do something about it.

Now, I propose three things that we could do. Because, as I suggested at the beginning, each one of us, hopefully, will suggest specific programs.

The first one is, I think we should start a magazine sometime next year. I know it is extremely difficult to start magazines now, but I think we need a forum. This magazine will be involved in investigative and speculative journalism, that will not only be responding but will be pro-active to the attacks. About five or six pages will be devoted to letters from the public. Let them write what they want to write.

I have been sending a lot of letters to the *Toronto Star* or *Globe & Mail* and only one has ever been published. So we need a forum. Many of us need that kind of forum. That magazine will be different. And I suggest that if you can be a founding contributor we can discuss after today how we can start that magazine. The name has not been chosen. We have not done the ground work, but I think we need something that we will call our own.

Some of the newspapers we have now from the community generally are only reacting to what is going on. Most of the time they don't even publish our articles. We need something like *McLean's Magazine*, or *Nairobi Law Monthly* or *Emerge* from the United States, or similar magazines. And I am proposing that that magazine start publishing sometime next year. Now, it may not come to fruition, but I lay it out as an idea of what we could do to respond to the attacks.

The second idea I have is that by next September 1995 I think we should start our own school, which may be called Centre for Legal Studies, where we will teach our own courses to the African-Canadians in law, journalism, private investigations, social science, so that we can staff our own institutions with the people we have trained. It is also an employment creation venture. And it would be also helping people from colleges and high schools to do something that will assist their community. Right now we don't have our own school where we can train our own intelligentsia. We need our own organic intellectuals. We will be looking at various proposals, and we will try to get funding from different bodies. And we can rent a school in the evenings, on weekends. We will be giving certificates.

We need to position ourselves for the 21st Century. We need to have our own expert witnesses in the courts to talk about the racial discrimination that we suffer. Right now we have no African-Canadians who are experts, who can be qualified as experts to talk about racial discrimination in the courts.

We don't have among racial minorities private investigators who we can send around to dig out information that will help our community.

We need more African-Canadian journalists who we can employ in this very magazine that we have proposed. As you know, most of the African-Canadian journalists now in the mainstream media started out at Contrast magazine when it existed. And the media has grabbed some of them. But some of them out there have not yet been grabbed.

I think this school I am proposing would do, in my view, a good job in training our own intelligentsia.

The third proposal is that we should start our own centre for collecting data documents on the experiences we suffer.

If you have been attending the hearings of the Commission on Systemic Racism, someone used to raise the question that what we are talking about are merely anecdotes. When you are talking about your experiences it is an anecdote, it is not evidence. So we need to collect data. We need to have this data bank whereby anyone who alleges discrimination may come and do research in that office and find out a pattern. And once we have a pattern we can present these patterns to the court, so that our experiences are not aberrations, they are not exaggerations, but our experiences. And we can co-opt this data from time to time.

The last proposal, which really is not a proposal but is already existing out there. There are some people who have formed the Caribbean-African Chamber of Commerce. There used to be a previous one but it has died out. But one has just been revived. This Caribbean-African Chamber of Commerce, I have the information here, you can talk to me afterwards, and you can become a member. We have the form here. It will be helping Africans in accessing loans, funds to start their own businesses. It will be providing information on how to get contracts from the government, how to network and so on and so forth, because you need economic power for political influence. No economic power, no political influence; no political power, no legal influence. We need to stand on our own feet economically. We need no longer be dependent on the handouts from the government. We can support ourselves.

Thank you very much.

- DR. MUNYONZWE HAMALENGWA

I now call upon Marlene Norbese Philip, whom I have already introduced. And I don't know what she is going to talk about.

MARLENE NORBESE PHILIP: What I thought I would do, as I often do, is start with two poems, which will take us back some at least fifteen to twenty years. And my talk today will actually go back some twenty years. I will be focusing on the struggles around the Immigration Act, because a great deal of what we are seeing actually is not new, has happened before. And there is a certain cycle. So what I am going to try to do is put a historical and somewhat theoretical approach to what I think is happening in Canada and why immigration is used as a mechanism.

The first poem has to do with the shooting of Albert Johnson, whom many of you will remember, by the police. It's called Black Man Dead: (Poems Read) [Not transcribed, speech missing].

AFUA PAM COOPER: What I want to talk about is strategies, or perhaps one strategy to deal with this, you know, attack on the Black community especially by the media, the mainstream media. And I suspected that something like this had taken place before or would establish -- I knew in the early 80's people like Al Hamilton and some other people had started a media watch, but I don't think it had flourished or continued. And now you said the Black Secretariat was involved in a media watch. Well, that's my proposal, that we set up a media watch called "Black Watch", if you will, as a watchdog committee to monitor the reportings, how the Black community is reported in the mainstream press. This would not be purely a group that reacts to whatever, to the statistics and the headlines -- the daily headlines of us on the front page, but would be more of a proactive group in the sense that it would give consciousness-raising seminars, educational seminars to media and other groups. That's not to say that the media needs to be educated, that it's educated, that it doesn't know what it is doing because it does know what it is doing. You know, this country, Canada, is a settler state. It was built on racism. It was built on the extermination of other peoples and the appropriation of land from these peoples, the Native Peoples. So it was built on white supremacy. So the media, the *Star*, the radio, the whatever, they know what they are doing. This has been going on since Day 1. So that's my proposal basically.

The reporting of Black people in the newspapers and so on as criminals, you know, as lazy, as

- DR. MUNYONZWE HAMALENGWA

people who don't want to work, is not something new. If you look at the press in the 19th Century, it's the same thing. You know Blacks are lazy, they have sex more than anyone else; they are prone to become criminals, black men want to rape white women. In the 19th Century Ontario press, even the liberal -- which was considered liberal then, the *Globe* which evolved into the *Globe & Mail*, would often repeat some of these sayings. It is not something new. I think it's time that we launch a consistent activity to stop and to counter what's happening to us. You know, I really feel it's not hard to imagine that Black people could be eliminated really in Canada, eliminating us through putting us in the prisons. I mean, the statistics for black people, black men in particular in Canadian prisons, it's just appalling when we make up less than six percent of the population. So we can be eliminated in that way, being put in prisons, being killed, having our children, as I mentioned in the letter that I sent to the share, in the behavioral classes in the schools. And this is where it happens. Because if the children are dropping out of school from, let's say, Grade 9 -- sixty percent of Black children do not finish high school, especially Black boys -- and so to me it's like an unholy alliance between the educational system and the prison system, because they leave high school unskilled, low formal education. What's going to happen to them? That's easy to guess, right. Then they end up in prison or in jail. You know, it's easy for me to imagine that we could be effectively eliminated, our physical presence erased and no one would say anything except us. So I am submitting that we start a Black Watch to be an effective force in the media to be responsible and accountable and sensitive in its reporting, on the so-called criminal activities in the Black community. That's my submission.

MUNYONZWE HAMALENGWA: The next person will be Kiki Roach. She will be talking about physical anhilation of our people.

KIKE ROACH: I am going to be talking about the police and the block to achieving justice in situations where the police commit crimes against innocent Canadians. And, basically, I am focusing on the police because the police are like the thin, blue line that encircles the whole society and keeps all under wraps, under control, well-documented in those not-so-secret files, and makes sure that the status quo basically is maintained. And so, in talking about this I realize that, you know, the trends that we are seeing now that we can observe now are trends that have been developing over hundreds of years. And really, what we are seeing in these situations is the outgrowth of things such as imperialism, things such as slavery, and that continued legacy that slavery has given us, as well as the legacy that the Anglo-American system of legal justice has given us.

So everyone of us in this room know that when it comes to that blue line, that blue line seems to encircle and tightly choke sometimes the poorest of the society. And we disproportionately tend to find ourselves in that class. But we can also note that -- just the fact that we are not Melanin-challenged, this is like a great sort of target find that's sort of on us, that can make it very easy for anyone of us, despite our educational background, despite our class background, to become targets to and victims of police brutality and police killings. So, as such, Black people in this country have always been on the vanguard, on the other side of changing those institutions, of bringing meaningful change to those institutions. And that's what I want to talk about a little bit now.

I think it's really important for us to understand the general sort of historical and social and economic situation that we are in that will give us insight. But we also need to get very, very specific, because, really, in all of these battles, all of the victories that we have ever won have not been in convincing the society that it is terribly faulted morally and things like that on a grand general philosophical level or metaphysical level or anything like that; it's being in the actual nitty-gritty of doing work around very specific cases that happen in society. Because we cannot really speak to people who, you know, who continually deny racism, and can't speak to them on that theoretical institutional level without bringing forth the actual sort of injuries that are committed and talking about those. So we need to know that history and we need to get very detailed about it. And that history has shown that there is just a long litany of names that I can ring them out to you who had been -- both men and women who had been attacked and assaulted and killed by the police.

It's very important for us to see what the pattern is in all of these situations, and then when you have realized what the pattern is, to then be able to come up with strategies and recommendations and proposals that will be effective. So one thing I will talk about is the community itself and how it responded to this kind of police brutality. But before doing that I will just talk a little bit about, what are some of the blocks to getting a situation where we can actually charge the police or hold them accountable for all the things that they are doing.

One of the major blocks is that the institutional machinery that is around, you know, keeping us in line is very, very formidable. And people fear it so; everybody fears it, it seems. And it's supported by so many branches, and such a complex working of chiefs, and commissioners and judges and prosecutors or even defense lawyers who all seem to be condoning racism.

Racism itself is not even seen as a crime. And that's probably one of the fundamental problems that we face, and will continue to face, is that racism is so inbred in our society that we just take it for granted. And as my father has pointed out numerous times it's much -- it is a complex and smoothly run system to make sure that you follow all of those traffic laws. And now they have instituted photo radars, you know, so they can catch everybody and bring in all the money that they want. It's much easier for a person to be punished for a traffic violation than it is for a person to be punished because they have denied the person a job, to a livelihood. It's much easier for a police officer to go and kill someone and be left totally unpunished, unaccountable, than it is for someone to go 200 miles over the speed limit.

So this is the kind of society that we are working with here. And this atmosphere of intimidation that is brought forth by all of these complex institutions, we have a silence of not only those within those structures but also of people outside of those structures such as the churches such as labour movements and unions and other institutions that have often failed to speak out when we have had this increasing rise of tension that Norbese Philips spoke of where nobody seems to be taking on the challenge to speak out against it. But more specifically, some of the blocks have been: in the past we had a situation where complaints against the police were all within the police institution. So here you are you have just been brutalized by a police officer and you have to go down to police headquarters and tell his brother one of his good buddies that he has just had a coffee with has beaten up on you. So obviously this doesn't engender a lot of trust in people. It's been very, very difficult to lay criminal charges on a police officer in such matters. And what really needs to be done is that when somebody is killed, which is the greatest crime that anyone could commit, or the greatest phenomenon that you could do is to end somebody's life. There has often been a situation where if you manage to lay a charge it's been something like criminal negligence, or some other such thing, whereas what we need is a first degree murder charge to be laid on the police officers so that we can bring into court all of the information, all of the testimony and so on that we need to hear, so that that truth can come out into the court. What happens when you don't have a first degree murder charge is that a lot of evidence, a lot of testimony and so on can be seen as irrelevant; you cannot bring that in formally into the court system.

Another thing is that instead of bringing criminal charges but realizing that people see and desire bringing enough pressure to say that, you know, we need some kind of remedy to happen here. What they do is, instead of having criminal charges, we will have an inquest. And an inquest is very useful in terms of us getting some information. At the end of the day, none of that information can then be used to lay criminal charges on the police officer. So all the information can come out, we can say how terrible something was and how -- and we can see how responsible some officers were in a particular death, but at the end of the day all we can say is, there it is, and they are still walking off scot free.

The other problem that we have had in general is that a lot of lay people have been kept totally ignorant of what their rights are in terms of their relationships with the police. And this can lead to a lot of abuse.

Within the police system we have seen the tendency of the police chief and commissioners to, once there is a new case that crops up with an alleged wrong doing, there is immediate support given to those police officers; without knowing any of the details, without knowing the circumstances or situations, immediately there is this support that comes out for the police officer. And the news media reinforces that report by giving information that is often favourable to the police and not at all impartial. And there is an immediate discrediting of the victim of that violence, and so that we hear that the victim is a crack head or he has had a long-standing criminal record and so on. And this makes people feel that, well, maybe he deserves to die anyway.

Then we have a situation where victims are threatened or intimidated, as I mentioned before, without even being allowed to lay a complaint. And there is a difficulty to find lawyers in this city who will take on that powerful institution. They are a handful. And they are being well stretched. Victims are often dissuaded by people in the legal profession from taking on the police. And the truth is that it is very difficult to take the case to a civil court and get any kind of remedy or justice because of the tight nature in which the court system and the police system work together. So these are some of the concrete blocks that we have that are work to prevent any kind of real justice from coming about.

But just to speak very briefly of the news media, and some of the things. I think that we should not just focus on the news media but also the entertainment industry as a whole, and whole institutions of representations of ourselves wherever we see it, whether it be in advertising, whether it be in the news media, whether it be in movies. Because, if you have noted lately, a new phenomenon is the video phenomenon. Everybody goes and spend their weekends watching videos from Blockbuster Video or these other places that have sort of descended in every neighbourhood. And the videos that you can find in there are ones in which Black men are incessantly degrading each other and killing each other, and the value of black life is totally absent. So that sort of sinks into the common imagination. And we find a situation where people can walk away and just think, well, hey, these people don't even care about each other's lives why should we be getting so upset when a police officer in the line of duty commit some supposed error. So we should look to the entertainment industry and be critical of that also. And I hope that some of us will get into that industry and take it over so that we can document our own real stories.

The other thing that the news media has done is to blow a violent crime way out of proportion. On occasion the Star has, twice I think, that they have actually reported that there has been no increase in violent crime over the last few years if you factor in the increase in population and so on. Yet, there is an incessant focus on those types of crimes, when in reality the majority of crimes are not really people holding each other up in shops and so on. And so that reinforcing in the public mind that we are living in a terribly dangerous, violent culture, where at any moment you could walk out and be held up against a wall by some strapping black man and we have all got to watch out is just false; it is just out of proportion. And the fact that Chief McCormack showed up at Vivi Lamonis' funeral also sent a very clear message to the melanin-challenged people that, you know, he was there to safeguard and protect them. Specifically because it's highly unusual for -- when was the last time that you heard of a police chief actually showing up at anyone's funeral aside from maybe a police officer. So it's very, very unusual.

Now, just to move in talking very specifically about some of the cases that we have seen. I won't go into detail about a lot of the cases, because, as we have seen, there is just so many of them. And in all of these cases we haven't seen a single conviction, we haven't seen a single firing of any of these individuals. In fact, some of them have been promoted and given their paid vacations. But what I want to say though is that despite those grim realities, we have, nevertheless been making tremendous progress. And I can say that I was fortunate enough where I was raised in a family where I basically learned to walk on demonstrations. And sometimes we feel the sense of, oh, well, maybe if I write a letter here, maybe if I show up with a placard here that's not really doing too much. But in fact if we look at the history we can see that, you know, we have been making incremental -- we have had incremental successes, even though we have not had right down to the line, the convictions that we want to see, which will be forthcoming.

In that I would say that community activism is the real solution to affecting any kind of positive and long-term change. And we have to be very careful because that element is being co-opted and that history is being buried. Recently the SIU, the Special Investigations Unit, which I will talk about a little bit, came out with a report. And it said in this report that the SIU was formed because they had a forum, a forum in 1988 and people came and made presentations and gave elaborate papers and so on, and expressing concerns and so on, and out of this forum that was, you know, funded by the government, the SIU was created. Well, in reality, that's not the way it came about at all. A lot of the activism came out really around the Albert Johnson case as Norbese Philip was talking about, around the Buddy Evans case. You had groups of people who formed the ad-hoc organizations to basically militate so that we could see some justice done in these specific cases. And those led to later - on the formations of groups like the Black Action Defense Committee, like the Women's Action Against Racist Policing Committee that developed out of the Sophia Cook incident. You had the Coalition for Police Reform, which members were formally part of a group called the Citizens Independent Review of Police Activities. Those are the kinds of organizations that failed to show up in the media in any kind of positive light, and that are constantly being maligned and attacked as a bunch of rif-rafs,and radicals and so on. But those are the groups that then bring about important structural changes. So we have had a situation where, out of that kind of agitation and militancy, from just, you know, people, that we have seen a situation where the complaints whole mechanism was moved out of the police departments. And now we have a separate and independent public complaints commission, with it's faults. But nevertheless that's a major move. We have seen a situation where we now are seeing that charges are being laid, and that those charges are more often charges of second degree murder instead of just the manslaughter or criminal negligence that we saw before. And we have seen the outgrowth of this Special Investigations Unit as well.

Of course, there are problems within all these outgrowths of remedies, but it's a significant change in development from a time when there was nothing, nothing would happen at all.

We have seen a situation where the SIU, for example has moved from being under the leadership of a man named Osler, who, in his wisdom, went behind everyone's back and made a secret deal with the police to then take any cases that came to the Special Investigations Unit, which is supposed to be a totally independent body, take any of those cases and turn the investigations back into the hands of police officers. This was the secret deal that later came out. And this was just phenomenal, you know. Because what we have learned is that it's in the investigation that the truth really comes out; it's the investigation that lays the foundation for everything else that's going to happen after that. So that's the key place where independent bodies need to be. And Osler wanted to make sure that that wouldn't happen. To now having Howard Morton, who is a man of a different stripe, who has a different relationship with especially the African-Canadian community and consults much more with this community, tries to have some bit of integrity in terms of making sure that it is in fact an independent investigation. And it's interesting that recently a group of people met with Mr. Morton, and he said, after giving them some information about some of the most heated cases at hand right now, he said, okay, I am giving you this information and I hope this means that you don't show up in front of my office with any placards.

It is important to note that those demonstrations, that public embarrassment of those officials, does have a real impact. And this is what is really important. We are now getting vital information that was before totally secret and hidden.

- DR. MUNYONZWE HAMALENGWA

I will just talk about a couple of cases that show that let us have some more insight and more of a door into how we are going to rectify this system, that has only been made available to us, basically, because of the Special Investigations Unit. One case is the Kenneth Allen case: a man who died in police custody. Through reports that came out from the Special Investigations Unit we learned that there was video tape recorded at one of the police stations that showed clearly -- that showed that this man, after they studied this case very, very closely was already lying down in a prostrate position, and he was dragged into obviously an unconscious state. He was taken into his cell where there was a video monitor monitoring the whole thing. And it was shown that this man was dragged into this cell already in an unconscious state with a billy club under his neck. This is how he was brought into the cell. He was left with his left prostrate sort of gagging for a few moments, and there was a significant gap of time in which this man was in obviously a very serious condition and no one made sure that medical attention was brought to him at all. And then it was later found that there were very, very grave bruises on his neck that could have engendered that kind of suffocation or inability to breathe that he later suffered from. He died in custody. That kind of information we would never have gotten if we didn't have the Special Investigations Unit brought in there.

The other case is the case of Ian Coley, whom you have probably read about in the papers. In the Ian Coley investigation we were able to sort of find out more about what was delaying the whole matter,and see that where some of the inability to actually carry out the proper work of the Special Investigations Unit is due to the fact that the police officers themselves refuse or very often resist sitting down in those interviews, which they are required to do under the Police Services Act and submitting to those Special Investigations Unit officer coming and documenting all of the important facts and factors following a wrongdoing. So in the Coley case we had a situation where even though Coley was killed on April 20th of 1993 it wasn't until May 25th of '94 that finally Constable Shank with his lawyer went to the Special Investigations Unit to have the required interview done. And he did this only because he wanted a promotion at work and wasn't being given it until he complied with this *Police Services Act*. So what we had here is a situation where Shank basically decided that, Oh, I am not going to listen to the *Police Services Act*, and I am going to fall back on the *Charter of Rights and Freedoms* which says, you know, I have the right to do this dilly dallying, you know. This is totally unacceptable and something that we have to combat. Because as a police officer you have to be held to a higher level of accountability. You are not just another citizen walking around in the street. You are given and entrusted with the ability to actually kill someone. And that is definitely something that has to be seen with a greater level of responsibility and accountability.

So these are some of the improvements that we have seen. But, as I mentioned, within the Public Complaints Commission we saw that there is some need for it to be improved because it was that other fiasco in the Audrey Smith's case, where they later discovered that one of the panel members who they appointed to look over the case was in fact somebody who is a family relations of the police officer involved in the matter. And it's beyond me how they couldn't have seen this before. It was the father actually of one of the police officers who was involved in the strip-searching of Audrey Smith on the street who was then put on a panel to judge whether any wrongdoing was happening. Audrey Smith comes back from Jamaica to endure this whole trauma again, and then the thing has to be postponed because they noticed that the father is there and that people would be upset.

The establishment thinking is predictable. Like, We need to hire some more so-called visible minorities. We need sensitivity training. If they maybe know something about Roti and Jamaican Patties, and stuff like that get into some Reggae maybe then -- wine a bit, then maybe somehow they will stop killing us. But these kinds of suggestions have often come from people who have never been involved in community activism and don't see that as the real force and having the real potential that it does. So we have to reject those kinds of suggestions and see instead the need for us to have grassroots people who are actually serving on the boards that are then going to -- like the Police Services Board and other boards that are going to control and be at a place where the rest of the police services are governed from.

We need to assume that there is racism involved in these cases, given the nature of our society. We should be thinking that maybe not all officers have to carry guns. There are many other countries where officers do not carry weapons. And although I have said that mere affirmative action is not the answer, we do need to see a situation where the officers do reflect the communities that they work with. But it's also important for us to -- the idea or suggestion was made that we need to document these cases. And I think it's important for us to document these cases of people who have been victimized within our community. But it's also very important to document those police officers who are involved in all of these activities.

We always hear what the possible criminal background is of any victim. We never hear what the background is of those police officers who are committing these crimes. And if we look at the situation of Lester Donaldson, a man who was disabled by the police, and then later on they went back to finish the job and killed him in his rooming house, we would see that Constable Deveney, David Deveney, who was acquitted of course, and walked out of the courtroom with a big cigar, we would see that he had a terrible record of racism and abuse, in which he had a file on him documenting the fact that he had a history of brutalizing and attacking people in the Black community. And actually, I believe that you had another client or acquaintance who was similarly attacked by Deveney. And it's allowing people like that to continue on that leads to these situations of death coming about, because the atmosphere is one in which it's totally acceptable.

So we need to have that documentation. And that sort of information should be made known to the public as well.

So while it is important for us to know that history, document it, it's also important for us to not only have, I think, things in the print media, but also use the power of the video and the film and so on to reach large numbers of people, and to document our own community activism and see what were the things that were effective, and build on those things in order to create strategies for the future. So I think it's really important that we note that embarrassing authorities does work, that community agitation is the only way that we have seen structural changes being effected. That kind of agitation or community support can take place in many different way, demonstrations is one way, but support to families and presence in the courtrooms and spokespeople in the media, and so on, are other ways of linking up with the lawyers in our own Black community and so on, and building that kind of political pressure then placed on people are other important ways. So we need to build, basically, on our own community institutions and traditions.

And I think I will turn it over now to my father who will talk a little bit more about how we can do that. Thank you.

- DR. MUNYONZWE HAMALENGWA

MUNYONZWE HAMALENGWA: I have to say one or two things about Charles Roach. And after he has spoken we will take some questions.

Charles Roach is a Renaiscence man. There is nothing Charles Roach cannot do. There is something engraved in my memory about Charles Roach. One time he invited me to his house, and I went there. And I didn't really know him at that time. But when I went there I found that he was playing a guitar with Lennox Farrel. And when these two connect on a stage to do something, they are a powerful, powerful pair. And I have never forgotten that kind of image that is still engraved in my mind about Charles Roach. He is an entertainer, he is a lawyer, he has fought many, many battles. And it's a pleasure to have Charles Roach here today.

CHARLES ROACH: I have to get up for a stretch. Thank you very much.

Just let me say what I am concluding with, just in case you have to go in the next two or three minutes.

I want to say that we need more people to be joining the Black Action Defense committee, so that we can institutionalize it, formalize it and have it upgrading in a manner which would make it even more powerful than it is now. There are some other groups that you can join, such as the Metro Coalition on Police Reform, of which many BADC people are members of. You can join that one as well. And there are a few others. But I want to talk about BADC and the importance of doing our activities through BADC.

Now, we did have a very nice historical background and some of the problems more recently have been stated by previous speakers. But as I look at you I can see so many of you that have been involved for so many years, for such a long time in the struggle against racism, so I don't have to be explicit in mentioning years so far as the points I am going to make.

Now, with respect to policing, policing is only one aspect of the struggles that we have. We have immigration problems, as has been mentioned before, and we have problems in the education system. In fact, in every institution, in every single institution, people of colour, poor people are faced with problems.

The reason that we, me and people like yourselves and the Black Action Defense Committee focus on the police is that, if you want to make any radical changes, any really different changes and you want to move to get those changes in place you are bound to be confronted by the police. There is no question about it, okay. If you want to make those changes but you are not taking any steps, you are writing documents or you are sending in briefs and so on, you won't confront them. But once you start mobilizing people, once you take them or move with people to any location, once you go outdoors, then you are going to be confronted with the police.

Our system is a liberal democracy, and they would permit you to write all kinds of things. Mr. Ruby, for example, writes wonderful things about the police and exposures and so on. We saw Alan's story, for example, exposing corruption in the newspapers, in the Star, over the Younger affair, which we didn't know. And when you file that out, nobody did anything about it at all. Weeks, months passed by and it was just dropped, because people are just afraid of the police. And nothing would have been done unless persons like myself organized to bring pressure on the attorney general and the solicitor general, to say, look, we have to have an inquiry about this, and mount demonstrations at police headquarters, saying 'Hit the road, Mack, and don't come back no more'. Those are the kinds of things that you are doing.

It seems to me that we don't all have to have the same organization, but it is the vanguard organizations, the activist organizations -- and when I say "activist" I mean mobilizing people, not just having progressive thoughts and writing things down. Those organizations are the ones that make changes.

Now, I say this on the basis of my observation, and trying in various kinds of ways to make changes. Although those organizing to make changes, they don't necessarily benefit directly from those changes.

For example, all of the things that happened in May 1992 when we had the fracas there on Yonge Street, arising out of that millions of millions of dollars was made available, or were made available to the community. But people down below didn't necessarily get that. Maybe a little bit trickled down to jobs, the Joy Programs and so on. But who is getting that money? We have the Commission on Systemic Racism that is put into place. Right now we are going to have a Black resources legal facility that is going to be put into place. The attorney general has already put that into place, and comes September that is going to be up and running. And then there are others who have been given contracts to do all kinds of studies and so on. And this is the way the thing works. Always when there is a shooting, or when there is a reaction of the people in the streets, like around Wade Lawson, for example, we have some kind of task force and we have all of those professionals, progressive people or people who are not part of that vanguard movement coming in and setting up all the tables and the graphs and all that kind of stuff, putting them on the wall, taking them down to Queen's Park and getting money for doing those things.

Well, that is a necessary process, and I respect that. But I think to get any kind of process going we do need this vanguard activism that we see the Black Action Defence Committee taking part in.

Now, the Black Action Defense Committee is really older than it seems to be, because it has changed it's name, really, basically, as the years go by. So we have had the Black Action Defense Committee since Buddy Evans, when we had the Committee for Due Process. And some of the same players are in there all the time, and even up to today.

And so, what they actually do is try to mobilize people. Unfortunately, they have not been able to attract middle class people, people who, for example, would come to OISE and study all kinds of things about police, education of police and so on, we have not been able to attract them. And I am just appalled that we have so many Black lawyers and so few who would want to identify with BADC, or who would go down there and help BADC.

Now, BADC is running on a shoestring, and it's an incredibly impoverished kind of organization. If you go in there you will see what is happening. But the strength of it is more in its moral force than in its physical organization. And its strength is not being afraid to confront the powers that be, and particularly the politicians. Because BADC doesn't necessarily confront the police. They very seldom do that. They go to the politicians; they go to Queen's Park to the people who are responsible. And so it is doubtful whether we would have any of these progressive changes that we have seen in the legislation without that kind of activity, very, very doubtful.

I feel that if we had more of our people who are better off or middle class people in the African-Canadian community involved in organizations like BADC, we would make a revolution here that you can't think of. But many of them feel that, alas, we have distance, we won't get ahead. I don't think that that is necessarily so. But it may be so to some extent, because this system does not like very revolutionary-minded people. This system does not like people who want to make reforms, radical reforms; it prefers to do things in a gradual, controlled kind of way, and it prefers to go through a kind of process. And so be it. But still, that does not prevent us from giving financial and moral support.

It is dangerous to some extent to get involved with BADC, because as Munyonzwe was just showing you the article about Arnold Minors, in which they said that he should not be a candidate for the police commissioner, or chief police commissioner, or chairman of the Police Services Board because he went to the BADC dinner, and he was photographed at the BADC dinner. So they say, he is being touted, we have got to cut him down quickly, and at the same time they are touting others.

I want to say a word about Fantino. I don't want to forget so I am going to interrupt myself to get into this.

We see now a move by Mr. Fantino, chief of police, to come back here. He has never moved his home, you see. He lives in a hotel in London. And his family is still here in this area and so on, and it's what you might call, a professional move that he made. And he has changed; he has changed somewhat, okay, than what he used to be, because he is a little bit more sensitive.

I have known this man for many, many years. Way back in the mid-seventies I actually sued him, and he was in court for brutalizing some of our clients. And then right now I have a law suit against him, and just last month we were down demonstrating with a number of people in front of the London Police Station for the kinds of violations of Black people's rights that he is committing down there.

There is a case called the Cy Campbell case. I don't have time to get into it, but this is where he is really very, very unfairly treated a particular person in such a way. The man has not committed anything, but he has lied on him, he has done everything to discredit this particular man. And the move is to get him back here.

Now, you know he is the man who was the mastermind in the frame-up of Dudley Laws. It started as an idea in his mind, and he got the consent of the Chief,and then he just structured it with a large amount of money; the RCMP was just brought in as a facade. But they were behind it.

So what we have is a move to bring him back, and he might be the favourite of the men on the beat. The technique of the present Chief has been very good for him. He has been able to get away with a lot of things that any other person would 'bite the dust' for. The present Chief has been able to get away with breaking the laws, with committing what I call offenses, you know, falsification of his resume, wearing the U.N. Medal of Honour, the U.K. Medal of Honour for the Korean War, when he had never been six thousand miles near the Korean theatre of war, you know. And he said, okay, when he was caught, "I will just take them off and I won't wear them again, but the Sheriff's Officer told me it was all right to get these", so he went and he bought them and he was wearing them. At a time when it would definitely be preferred, if you are a veteran, you see, if that was on your resume. And we know that he conspired to destroy evidence in the Younger case. We know he also countenanced that his officers do not comply with the SIU and the Police Act, the provisions that officers must report to the SIU any activity that they did, or if they wanted to claim the protection of the Charter, they could resign and claim that, but if they want to stay on the force, they must comply. But he countenanced the non-compliance and so on. So he is really, in many, many, many ways, he has broken the law and not upheld the law.

Now, somebody like, you know, Roy Williams, for example, you remember he had to step off, because of some bylaw with a house? I don't know if you know the case of Mary Endolym, who is a Black commissioner of the Peel Police Region. Well, she said we have to be guarded because some police officers would lie to back up their escorts and so on in cases where there is accusations of brutality. For saying that, she was -- well, actually, she was charged. It was an administrative type of thing. And we had to represent her and fight to make sure she did stay on there. And you know how many of our people who have attained any kind of position have been taken to task. Whether it would be Alvin Curling in the .... affair, when he had lots of distance. One day he was in his limousine, the next day he was walking. We see Zanana Akande, a wonderful, wonderful woman, whom we are all proud of. When she speaks out, when she does things, they use other ways of partitioning her, that she got so disillusioned with the whole mess of politics. Okay? And we see it in many, many other cases: Carlton Masters; we are seen -- now they are trying to do it with other people, and eventually brought down -- tried to bring down our real civil rights leader, Dudley Laws. Because my impression is, having been in this area since the mid-fifties, that Dudley has certainly been an individual who has devoted more of his life than anyone of us to see that we have proper policing. And for that reason he was framed up and tried and thrown in jail. He still has another case coming up arising out of that last one. Two other charges were mistried. They pertain to the same facts, but in October he has to go again for trial on those, while he is appealing those that he was convicted on. So they are really putting him through the wringer.

So what I would like to see is this organization called the Black Action Defense Committee get a tremendous amount of support. And don't fall into the trap, when they say, "Does Dudley Laws speak for you?" Don't fall into that trap at all. It's not a valid question at all. The question is: What is the issue? Do you agree or disagree with this issue? Let's talk about the issues.

And so, what we need is to see that organization funded properly. It cannot get government funding, because if it does its rhetoric will have to be toned down, you know. Some name that is being mentioned, will not be mentioned, or whatever it is. So once you are being funded you cannot be a vanguard agency. We do need funding for other kinds of agencies, subsistence agencies, maintenance agencies, and sporting agencies, and all those other kinds of agencies. But with an agency like this it has to speak out against government. And it cannot bite the hand that is giving it money, you see. So it has to get the money from ourselves.

And we have to be -- we have to speak up and defend it. Just speaking up and defending BADC in itself alone is a wonderful kind of thing.

If we had in BADC the forces to do the volunteer work and so on, what we would most likely take on is many of the things we are talking about. I don't see the necessity of forming any new organizations. I don't see the necessity of splintering, and we have thousands -- the Black community is very varied. So if other people want to form this, I will fight for their right to form it, although I don't see the necessity if we have one organization.

The reason for that is that, it may not be necessary, or it may even be cuddling things, unless there is some kind of working together, and saying, okay, we want to deal particularly with media and we want to deal particularly with something. But BADC has dealt with media and image. BADC is the one who, week after week, after week, had the demonstrations about "Show Boat". You are aware of that. BADC has been involved in immigration matters and has been supportive of those people there. BADC has been involved in supporting other groups like the Chinese community, the Hispanic community, and some of the other groups, the Palestinian community, and the Sikhs and so on in their various troubles. And BADC has been involved in health care issues, and education issues. It's best known for the police issue, because the police feel as though people are afraid of the police. But I want to tell -- I have a little bit of story I will tell you. The police are more afraid of you than you are afraid of them.

Sometimes you go into this great, big temple they have down there, you know, the Police Headquarters. They have built it in such a way that it will intimidate you, you see. And if you go in there you are going to see the Chief, or you are going to the Board or anything, you go through a kind of thing there. And if you are not used to it and doing it a lot you will certainly be intimidated. But a little story I want to tell you is a story that happened to me just yesterday. Lance phoned me and told me, Oh, the police are harassing the lady. They are coming to her door and knocking her door and so on, and I think the best thing for us to do is just find out what they want. And if they want to interview her, I will send her down to your office. She came down to my office and we made an arrangement for the police to be there in the presence of somebody, you know. Actually, they wanted to serve her with a summons on something. And they did serve her with the summons. But when the two officers, the plain-clothes officers came to my office, I went out and I greeted them, because I always like to greet people when they come in, you know. There is no personal animosity, it is just the principle. Okay? But I could see the officers, I could see that they were scared. So I put them into a boardroom and I sat them down, and then I went to another room, got the lady and I sat her down. And I say, very well, gentlemen, what would you like? And the officer took out his book or his paper that he had and he started reading. And the manner in which he was reading I could tell -- I was thinking, I wish I could put this man at ease. But I couldn't. And eventually they were glad to leave quickly.

So I am going to tell you that we don't have to be afraid, we don't have to be afraid at all. And most of the times courage is only speaking out when we see things going wrong.

MIGUNA MIGUNA: Munyonzwe, I think we need to mention that we have an afternoon session, that they don't have to feel that they have to leave immediately after this.

MUNYONZWE HAMALENGWA: Dudley Laws is coming in the afternoon. We are going to break slightly after one. And in the afternoon we have Dudley Laws, he promised to come, at two o'clock. And we have Norman Otis Richmond here, and we have MigunaMiguna, and we have Colin Brown. I saw him not long ago. We have people like Bev. Folkes, who have been dealing with the system for a long time. They may have comments rather than questions. So we invite your questions or comments.

MARLENE NORBESE-PHILIPS: Can I ask something of Charles, if that's allowed.

MUNYONZWE HAMALENGWA: Sure.

MARLENE NORBESE-PHILIPS: Explain a bit more when you talked about activist organizations -- which I totally agree with -- activist organizations making changes on the ground. I wonder if by the same token some of those changes don't necessarily spill over into other areas unless there is also an active -- like, for instance, the fact that BADC may get something done say around the police or even help, doesn't necessarily spill over into education. I don't know if you want to sort of speak to that?

CHARLES ROACH: Yes.

MARLENE NORBESE-PHILIPS: And I knew that you weren't saying that those groups shouldn't exist.

CHARLES ROACH: Yes, yes. There is no question that when you are talking about human rights there is a kind of benefit that everybody has, and there is a kind of working together at all the various levels and types of organizations. I wanted to make that clear. I am not saying that it's just an activist organization that is needed. Now you need organizations to preserve the gains that you already have, you see, and you need organizations to work in other areas.

I wanted to just say though, that whatever gains that BADC would make in the field of policing, or immigration or whatever it is would also have a spill-off or ripple effect on many, many other institutions. I can see you have that, because once we are present and they know that we are ready to speak out and so on, they would pay more attention.

For example, May the 2nd, 1992 was about -- what was that about, Raymond Lawrence and the case in California.

MARLENE NORBESE-PHILIPS: Rodney King.

CHARLES ROACH: I was not in the city at that time; I was in Savannah, Georgia, so I missed all of that. But that has had an effect in many, many fields, you see. And the effect is not only on policing, but it had gone in through the whole justice system, you know, the prisons and so on. The Systemic Racism Commission is studying the prisons, and they are studying even situations of handling -- apparently behaviour in schools, how you deal with high school students and junior school students, how you bring them into the system. It's very broad and wide-ranging. It goes into parole, it goes into job situations for released prisoners and all that type of thing. And I think too that it goes into education fields, more people in the legal field, and affirmative action everywhere. So we are quite sure that once we break open a civil rights issue anywhere, whether it's like what you are doing and what you have done in the PEN situation, that has wide-ranging effects. And what we have to do, who are not working specifically in one particular field, like if you are not working specifically in the literary field like you do, Marlene, and if you have a gain in there somewhere, we should be sensitive and quick enough to pick up in other fields so that we could re-duplicate those kinds of victories, you see.

MUNYONZWE HAMALENGWA: My friend there.

UNIDENTIFIED SPEAKER: Mr. Roach, you did mention about BADC and it's activist role in the society. For some reason, I realize that BADC has to be able to reach, as you mentioned, the middle-class Black community. Do you have any idea as to how BADC is making efforts to reach that middle class. It does appear to me that the issues that you are dealing with, particularly police brutality, is one of the major problem we have in society. However, we are unable to have Black activists or the middle-class Blacks in society to really make a conscious effort to coming out and helping out. Do you have any suggestion of any way or method of reaching mainstream Blacks? They are there, and maybe we could provide some level of assistance.

CHARLES ROACH: It is a class problem. It's definitely a class problem. The other day I was on a radio program. It was, you know, those talks shows in the middle of the night, after twelve midnight, you know, the time that we can get on the radio sometimes. Anyway, they were talking about community leadership.

I am telling you this story to illustrate the problem that you have there. So a man phones and says, well, Dudley Laws, I saw him on television with another Jewish guy. And the Jewish guy talked circles around him. We need university graduates, and we need people like yourself. He was talking about me. Yes, Man, to lead a thing like BADC. So I said to the man, I said, what's your name? He said, eh, eh, eh, he says, what do you want to know that for. I said, what's your phone number. He said, you want me to give my number on the air. I said, okay, never mind. I said, this is the problem. That in effect is the problem. You have a person like Dudley Laws who is manifest. He is saying what he is saying and he is right there, okay? Not just Dudley Laws. But we have Akua Benjamin, Dari Mead, Tidy Francis, the whole lot of those people. All the people on the BADC executive are pretty much the same, okay. But just to bring it here, because the media has focused on them so much. So I say, if you want to be a leader in this field you have got to be willing to say who you are, and you have got to be available. I said to him, I am speaking to you, my name is Charlie Roach, my home telephone is in the phone book and my office telephone number is in the phone book, and I have to come open. You have to be totally open in order to lead. You can't lead and be worried about your job, your promotions and all these types of things. So we have few people in a position to lead a vanguard organization. Martin Luther King could do that because he was independent. He was a church minister and he milked the SCLC which supported him. And he went out and raised a lot of funds. We don't know about this, but Martin Luther King was one of the greatest fundraisers ever. He raised millions of dollars from unions and other people who wanted to save their consciences, you know. And he was able to be independent. So that's a problem. If you are a civil servant you won't be expected to come out. It's not the role of a civil servant.

If you were working in some situation where you had to be accountable to your organization, you cannot come out. So a few of us, like myself, I have been all my adult life been independent, because I worked for myself and have my own business. But even so, they tried to kick me out of the Law Society. Still so, they schemed and tried to entrap me, like in certain cases and so on. So there is always a problem. So this is why middle class people would find it very difficult, unless they are completely out of that system. And they are what you call revolutionary intellectuals. It's very difficult for them to be involved in that situation. Because, the tactics are not acceptable, the tactics of, let's say, demonstrations, marches. They will go with delegations and briefs. Those other kinds of tactics are not the methods used by those people who have gotten a piece of the pie, you see.

MUNYONZWE HAMALENGWA: Bev. After Bev. it's this gentleman here.

BEV. FOLKES: I just want to express to the panel there my frustrations dealing with the justice system. I just sometimes feel like a voice crying in the wilderness. But there are so many injustices that we come across day by day. One of the things that I haven't .... in the Black community, is that we have had to take funds from the government, Charlie, because that's the only way we were able to do any work, because of the system.

MUNYONZWE HAMALENGWA: Maybe we should introduce Bev. Bev is the director/chairperson of the Black Inmates and Friends Assembly (BIFA), the only Black oriented group or organization helping Black prisoners.

BEV. FOLKES: But one of the things that I think is really, really needed, is for some lawyers -- and it has to be Black lawyers or lawyers of like-mind who can do some pro- bono work, because there are no funds to do it, to do some test cases.

I just want to point out a couple of things that I have seen happening in the prison system. Right now we have a real marriage between the Parole Board and Immigration. And citizens are being allowed to make deals with the Parole Board: I will go home to my country of origin if -- I mean, you want to get out. You are not going to get paroled because you are a threat to the Canadian society, but in order to get out, if you are prepared to make a deal, the Parole Board will say, okay, you are opting for this. It is not a deportation per se, but it is a question of, I can -- if I can go home I can be paroled. But I go home and remain there until my sentence is satisfied. Then you are free to come back. But I am sure there will be hurdles to come back. So you are not deported, you have not lost your citizenship, but you are allowed to do this.

MARLENE NORBESE-PHILIP: Are these landed immigrants or citizens?

BEV. FOLKES: These are citizens. So you are not being deported, you have not lost your citizenship, but you are being allowed to do this. It is illegal, it is immoral. But I can understand an inmate that is sitting there for seven, eight, eleven years. Right now, the same person to whom I spoke earlier in the office, she is finally granted parole, but she stays here until immigration takes her. She is not a citizen, I must say that.

The other problem we are having -- we had one of these prisoners -- we had a man who the police had taken in, charged him for obtaining a car through fraud. The man obtained a bank loan, bought his car, and for whatever reason the police decided that this is what he had done. They had him in jail. The courts had granted bail to this man. His relatives came five times to bail him and was told, we have no Justice of the Peace (J.P.). We had the dentist's case at Kingston Penitentiary (K.P.), whereby this young man was killed. And it is very clear that he was killed by correctional staff. When I was called immediately after his death I was told it is use of force. Now, they are trying to put that aside. And all the inmates who were there, these inmates have just been transferred all over the place, put into segregation in Milhaven, deported. All the evidence -- all the witnesses are gone. An inquest is supposed to come up. The mother is trying to get a civil action going against the correctional staff. But the system is pushing this inquest. They had their own people that they got together, who in turn did some kind of study on this whole thing. So if you ever see what we have on this young man, it is totally different from what we were given by the authorities. No J.P. to even take the charge. Finally, one J.P. was forced into a corner, a Black J.P. by the way, was sort of forced into a corner to take the charge, they are asking that this case not be held in Kingston but in Toronto. And that's the big fight. And we all know, I suppose, that Kingston is founded on the prison system, more or less. So I don't know what justice could be had there.

The man about the car, somehow one night after we opened up his case in the prison system, he is gone at midnight, no charges, no charges at all. We had people sitting in there the police brought in on charges that they had already served time for and had already paid some fines and something. By the time an investigation goes through this person is out of prison, vanishes. So we really need -- in this community we really need our own people to stand up there and do something.

I mean, I understand a need for money, but God, something has got to give. I am frustrated. I have just reached the point where I am ready to pack up and go back home. I have reached that point in my life, and I am being very, very honest with you. I have never seen so much injustices in my life.

I appreciate the work that is being done by BADC. But maybe one of the things that needs to be done, Charlie, is different sectors of BADC working in different areas. There is too much time, with the same people doing the same things without the expertise to do it. And I think maybe this is what is required.

on the petition, and so on, I endorse it wholeheartedly. But may I suggest that we go one step further. And when Parliament resumes we start organizing from now, when parliament resumes we march on Parliament Hill, as Charlie has done in the past.

And I don't have a lot of time to do some of these things, but whatever I can do to help, I will help. But I need help.

We have talked about people in the prison system. I got some stats. from Correctional Service of Canada, that shows where we are 2.43 percent of the total population of Ontario, and we are 9.7 percent in the prison system in Ontario.

We did an informal survey at the Metro East the other day, this young lady here did the stats. for us, Dianne, and what we found was 55 percent of the Black inmates are in fact Jamaicans, but we have also found that we are the majority of the Black community. And funny enough, the next highest amount of Black inmates are Canadian-born. So they won't be able to deport what they perceive to be the problem. But we have to deal with it. And I think we have to deal with our own people at a level of prevention also, not just secondary or tertiary, but before we seek an end to this.

We will have to work with our youth.

MARLENE NORBESE-PHILIP: Bev., could you just explain. You said 55 percent of the inmate population of Blacks in the prison system ---

BEV. FOLKES: In one particular prison.

MARLENE NORBESE-PHILIP: Are Jamaicans.

BEV. FOLKES: Yes.

MUNYONZWE HAMALENGWA: After this gentleman is Enid. And after Enid is, what's your name?

UNIDENTIFIED SPEAKER: It's Howard.

BEV. FOLKES: I am sorry, those we interviewed, of which was two hundred and seventy something.

UNIDENTIFIED SPEAKER: Were you 100 percent sure that they were Jamaicans?

BEV. FOLKES: Madam, I am not even sure who gave birth to them.

UNIDENTIFIED SPEAKER: There are people who parade as Jamaicans.

BEV. FOLKES: I am very aware. I do know that.

UNIDENTIFIED SPEAKER: Excuse me. I know that you were planning to take this break within fifteen or twenty minutes. So excuse me. But the last time I saw Charlie Roach was at L. Donaldson memorial service. And I would like to preface what I am about to say by telling you that the Al Hamilton Music and Theatre Workshop opens within three days at the Lionheart Studio right in the heart of Kensington Market.

Now, you talked about people being politicized at the grassroots level. Any of us who are over forty have already had that. The middle class Blacks that you are talking about reaching can be reached through theatre, music, drama, by school children, by professional artists, and gain their attention and let them know that this is going on. We would like to have Charlie and his organization sanction us to spread the word the way we do. We are street fighters and activists for forty years who have never been called on: an author, a musician, a music director and a music editor. But I have never joined forces with anybody. All I want is the sanction to spread the word the way we do, through art, literature and music and our talent. Because we are reaching a lot of middle-class Black people and others who send their kids to this school. And they want to know, but nobody wants to pick up a Share, if he is a civil servant, and hear that Charlie Roach is beating somebody's door down because the police are out in full force. If we can help, we would like to. And there are other organizations around this entire city waiting to do the same thing. And we can't hide. There is nowhere to run.

I once had a column in a newspaper magazine called "Where to go is what to do". I really believe that that's what we must do. And that's all I really want to say. I am pretty happy that this is all taking place at this time. So don't worry, we will be there to help you and support you by spreading the word, through protest and through music. And when we play the drum you know what happens, the police have heart attacks.

MUNYONZWE HAMALENGWA: Enid.

ENID LEE: Two general comments I hope will help in forming a strategy that we come up with today. And one has to do with questions of history, both alluded to by Norbese-Philip and Kike.

The first is documenting what has in fact happened. There is a general wastefulness in our community, as far as I am concerned. And we are always starting as though it is for the first time. It is like trying to write an essay, and every time we just go back to the first page. So up till today, we will say to ourselves, okay, what we are going to do -- how does it connect with what has gone before, and build. This is one.

And the second thing in the wastefulness, we need to use all the scraps and the pieces. Look at the purse here, it's made of scraps, scraps, you see, a scrap of leather, a scrap here. It is an African-Canadian, you know, you know his work. But it is made of scraps. And he says he doesn't throw anything out. We do that in our community with each other. And I am really saying here today, don't let's throw out any of the scraps, even if they are ill formed, even if they are not perfect. But we need to do this building work with this scrap to save this scrap. As middle class as it may seem on the surface, it might be used appropriately to do the work. I just want to say that because the wastefulness is great and the work is very big.

And we tend to think somewhat in our community in terms of shortage. And there are two things that we are not short of: we are not short of work, so there is plenty room for all of us. And nobody is going to bite us. And we definitely not short of people. But it's how to use those scraps. That's all I want to say. And I think the panel has made some excellent points. I hope we will take history and current scraps into account.

- DR. MUNYONZWE HAMALENGWA

MUNYONZWE HAMALENGWA: Let me just interject on that point regarding the falsification of history that Kiki just mentioned.

This Special Investigation Unit was really brought about by people like Charles Roach working in groups like BADC. But because none of us have documented the role of BADC, the role of Charles Roach, the role of Marlene and all the other people. There is no documentation so there is no information, so people can create their own history and say the SIU was created by these guys. So I endorse what you are saying a hundred percent.

ENID LEE: And a lot of the documentation is in different people's basements and files. We do have collections from newspapers.

KIKE ROACH: And so many of us have kept clippings from different events in the community.

ENID LEE: So we must keep that in mind.

MUNYONZWE HAMALENGWA: Exactly.

KIKE ROACH: And I forgot to mention that the SIU really came about in the wake of the death of Wade Lawson. It was after those intense protests that brought out actually thousands of people were coming out in that time, and it was during the winter. But thousands of people were coming out. And it was in the wake of that that we had the formation of the SIU.

MUNYONZWE HAMALENGWA: And you also imagine that a lot of our Black men have been shot by the police. There is no book by a Black lawyer, a Black author documenting all the deaths, in a book form tying this issue together. Nothing.

UNIDENTIFIED SPEAKER: Good time for you to do a book.

MUNYONZWE HAMALENGWA: I have just been busy doing my own, and it's right here. All the documents important in my life are in this book. We need a young student to write a thesis on this, you know, police reaction to this and so on and so forth. My brother over there.

UNIDENTIFIED SPEAKER: I just want to respond to comments about prisons. I work within the correctional system, and it does bother me to see the amount of Blacks that are imprisoned. Actually, I was in the Don Jail a few days ago -- I normally work in probation and parole, but from Monday I will be -- I don't know how long I will be attached, but I will be working directly in the Don Jail and mostly around the Black prisoners, because the report that came out on systemic discrimination, they are going to shift most of the Blacks within the system, within the Don Jail and the Hamilton Detention Centre where most of the problems are.

I don't think that's the solution. There are inmates who are Aboriginal who have been pushed the worst, even lost ... of the prisons.

systems for our offenders instead of putting them in those jails. I think the system has failed us. I think we are all just like how they had us on slave ships before, I think they are warehouses for our people. I mean, there are so many young people here under thc age of thirty, but if you go into the jails there, most of our Black young men are in there and it's a problem.

I deal with them and I have a lot of difficulties because of them.

CHARLES ROACH: It really could be a wonderful situation to have Black youngsters who are in jail if we could use that to give them a university-type education. Because they are going to be in there. And we just have to have those programs. Maybe what we should be doing is agitating to get programs where we can have teachers go in there and have classrooms and so on. Malcolm X raised his level to post-graduate standards. I mean, not officially, but by just studying in jail. There is nothing like having a captive audience.

BEV. FOLKES: Charlie, there are teachers in the prisons. However, it's just not enough. And furthermore, these teachers are coming from the various boards of education.

KIKE ROACH: They are trained in the ways of the system.

MUNYONZWE HAMALENGWA: Okay. We will take two more questions. And some of these issues are coming up in the afternoon as well, and they are interconnected. And Miguna Miguna will be there, Normal Otis Richmond, Colin Browne and Dudley Laws. We will take that gentleman's question and that gentleman behind there.

UNIDENTIFIED SPEAKER: I would just like to comment on some of the things that I hear coming up from various panelists.

It seems to me that one of the common things I keep on hearing is the building of institutions, and building up institutions that are already in place, and gaining some sense of self-reliance, instead of looking towards other institutions which are obviously failing us.

One of the observations that I have made come from realizations that have happened to me personally, is that we really can't trust or expect institutions that are created by this society that are run by white Canadians, that are created for white Canadians. We can't expect them to serve us.

On of the things I would like to ask that the panelists comment on is trying to find the resources within our own community, specifically our youth, which are, as you can obviously see, aren't really represented here today, and tapping into those energies which are out there, to start allowing our youth to take control of their own lives and their own future in regards to their survival in this country and in this time.

Perhaps if we could hear some suggestions on how institutions which are already in place might be able to reach the youth in places where they are already occupying now, perhaps through music, concerts, sports. These are the things that our youth are interested in and are heavily influenced by. Yet, when I, myself go to these other places where youth congregate and come together with one another very rarely are we seeing the faces within the room there trying to institute some sort of political activism within our youth today.

MUNYONZWE HAMALENGWA: Well, for myself I just want to say that two days I attended this founding of the Caribbean and the African Chamber of Commerce, and the keynote speaker there was Zanana Akande. And she said that there is billions and billions of dollars from government contracts, and the African-Canadian community is not benefiting from those contracts. So the money is out there. And Canadians or permanent residents of this country there is no reason whatsoever why we should not benefit from those contracts that are awarded by government, both provincial and federal.

So while I would support the idea of generating resources from our own community, there is no reason why we must not benefit from our citizenship in Canada by being awarded those contracts. So we have to access those contracts. Zanana emphasized that the same people year after year get these contracts, the same people. Corporations that make two billion dollars in profit, they get these contracts. Why can't we?

The reason why the Caribbean and African Chamber of Commerce has been set up is to try to access those contracts and grants and so on, because we are entitled to them. We may as well benefit from our existence in Canada. It's not like we should be treated as third tier citizens. We belong to this place and we are entitled to these resources.

UNIDENTIFIED SPEAKER: Let me respond. I agree with you wholeheartedly. What I was trying to focus in on was more the human aspect. I am concerned about our youth. Why are they expressing themselves through violence. And very many of them are becoming apathetic towards the system which they realize isn't created for them or intended to benefit them. But I sense that there still is some sort of willingness among them to fight and to challenge this system and the status quo. But they really don't have any sort of way to funnel their energy.

KIKE ROACH: I think that this calls attention back to the point of what we were talking about earlier in terms of institutionalizing or, you know, solidifying the kind of potential that we see coming out of groups like the Black Action Defense Committee.

I think that youth will gravitate towards organizations which they see to be effective, to be established, to have branches that they can come into. But if we have just an assemblage of people who are continually sort of working on an ad hoc basis to respond to the health crisis, immigration, police and so on it won't do. And if we continually placing a lot of stress on just a few of the individuals there is no way that we can build up that kind of solid organization that will then attract other, because the success of that organization will be well known and widely recognized and respected.

So I think that I agree with you, that there are a lot of people who are out there who could be very politicized and radicalized precisely in those moments when their best friends are killed by the police, or when they themselves are being harassed daily in various different situations, in social situations very often.

I think that we have to create different forums though, where those kinds of discussions can take place, because I don't think that they can take place when people are liming, or they want to just listen to some music or play sports, or things like that. I think that those can be positive sort of other things, activities that people can get involved in.

But if we want to talk about how to challenge the society, how to create a space for ourselves where we can really fully developed, I think we have to be serious about it, and we can't just say, okay, well, let's organize some dance or something like that, because people will not talk about these issues in advance. They won't talk. We have to get them in the moments when they themselves are being harassed, in the moments when, you know, just in the wake of the death that has happened. And it's through having those -- you know, I saw a lot of students and young people, people in the hostel who would never come out to anything, would never be political about anything. They were there when Wade Lawson died and there was a committee that was formed around him. But the problem is, we need to sustain that kind of interest and be able to figure out ways of chanelling that interest into doing other things, like, say, let's take up a video camera, let's make something, let's document our own history, let's have other kinds of forums when we can reach out to other youth and become really more politicized about these things and be able to develop strategies that are ongoing and long term, for people to address them.

So I think that, just to lead back into the question of talking about strengthening, those organizations have already been there. Because if we don't have the leadership in terms of people who are middle-aged people or older people then it won't, it can't trickle down.

MARLENE NORBESE-PHILIP: Following from what Bacchus talked about prevention, it is extremely important. I think that's what we are talking about. I don't think we can afford to wait for more deaths to get to our young people. Okay. Though they will happen and yes we have to capitalize on that, you also are very right in terms of when people are partying. Because when I took this out at Caribana time and tried to get signatures people did not want to talk to me about racism, because they were there to free-up. And that was a very good lesson for me.

But what this gentleman talked about, the music, there are already in place fresh arts or fresh starts. There are a number of organizations that are hitting young people, the move for black focused schools. And that is where we are going to begin to see changes. If we can get that on the road -- and one last point, one idea I have had every summer. And I send my kids away to camp now and then. Here is this wonderful country. We are a people of the land from Africa. I am not in social work, but those of you out there. One resource is to get our kids out of the city, on to the land. We can work with Native People, our own leaders from Africa, to begin to root ourselves through this land. Because the way whites have dealt with this land is not the way Natives have dealt with this land. And there is a resource there for us.

So I think there is a lot of stuff there we could do. And things are happening.

ENID LEE: And I think because those camps have actually happened. But, again, if you have a situation where people don't know. I know at least three of those have focused on Black youth. Just a minute so I make the point.

MUNYONZWE HAMALENGWA: I don't want to get into this afternoon session. So let's have a brief question from that gentleman. Then we will go for lunch and come back. This will be repeated in the afternoon. I am sorry.

UNKNOWN SPEAKER: The organizers of this forum should be commended. And all the presenters, I think they did a wonderful job. About what Charlie was saying. I was looking, please, to mention his cause when he has to go to court to beg a judge to ask policemen to behave. They should be thrown out at that very time. And I want to know, how can we help to prevent that type of thing. Whether it is demonstrating against him or whatever. I am going to be short.

Is there anyway the change that's made to good seeds.

CHARLES ROACH: You know, in Black language, "bad" means "good".

UNIDENTIFIED SPEAKER: The other thing too, you mentioned about the middle class joining. I would say, forget about lower, or upper, or middle class. It's not the class you belong to, it's the quality of your dedication and your courage, or solidarity. So we will come back after lunch and continue.

MUNYONZWE HAMALENGWA: Before you go for lunch, I want to emphasize that we hope these proceedings will be transcribed and that there will be follow-up contacts. And we hope you can give us your names and addresses and phone numbers. And we will contact you regarding follow up meetings and suggestions and so on.

There is a petition that you can sign outside. And please be back here about two o'clock.

MARLENE NORBESE-PHILLIP: If anyone wants a copy of the petition and thinks that they can get people, I have several copies here I can let you have.

MUNYONZWE HAMALENGWA: I want to thank all the speakers, please. Two o'clock. Be back at two o'clock.

--- LUNCHEON RECESS.
--- RESUMED.

MIGUNA MIGUNA: Thank you very much for coming back within an hour. I think we will get enough time to basically go through everything that we have to go through.

My name is Miguna Miguna, and I am going to chair this session. I will also say my piece before I give the opportunity to my colleagues here to say something to you.

To my right, to my extreme right is Otis Richmond. He is a writer and a broadcaster, he is a community worker and activist for a long time in this city. He will be speaking I don't know on what, but certainly on things that pertain to what we are here for.

And next to me is Colin Browne. He is a lawyer and community activist, and he has not divulged his topic as yet.

And to my left is Dudley Laws, who needs no introduction, who will obviously be talking about things that pertain to the community and on how we can empower ourselves, and keep on the struggle which ultimately will get us where we want to go, which is unencumbered liberation in all aspects.

It's quite obvious from the previous speakers in the morning that the history of our struggle is a long one. It has been a very long, long record history. And it's a history that is splattered with a lot of sweat and blood, a lot of anger and frustration and anguish, but also a history that has within it seeds of victory and success here and there. And it's those seeds that we should water so that they grow.

It is upon that struggle, the struggles that we have had actually that this meeting today is taking place.

Before we had this meeting I had several conversations with Munyonzwe. That was just before the so-called controversial Writers Through Race Conference that took place in Vancouver. I attended that conference. And we were talking about how we can deal with the media, how we can deal with the attack that has obviously been there for a long time. And we decided it would be good to have proactive seminars such as this, or meetings, where we come together and strategize together as a community, where, regardless of our political affiliations or whatever we identify as a community under attack. And that is what is happening today.

You may belong to the BADC, the Black Action Defence Committee, you may belong to other numerous groups in the city. That doesn't prevent us from working together. You may perhaps, after the end of the day, join the BADC or join other groups. That's very good. We can also continue to work as individuals.

I personally double as a lawyer and a writer. I have not done my Bar, I am doing my Bar this summer. And I have two books out, and I just completed a novel yesterday. And I am going to read a prologue of the novel and then I am going to say something small before I relinquish the reigns of power to my colleagues.

Now, my novel is called "Toes Have Tails". Toes, the toes that are on our feet, they have tales to tell, they have stories to narrate. And my novel is narrating such a story. And there are mainly two characters, the narrator and another character, both African refugees in this city. And the narrator is talking in the prologue, or maybe the "toe" of the narrator is talking to be more appropriate.

"Scratch, scratch. I scratch my big toes and follow the sloping along the meanders of the Nile up to Bel Al Gazar, where you commune with the Nubian rule elders before the long trek. The tedious migration south to the pitch blue waters of the Nile, through Gondokoro, where Nikan and Newel ripped open a chasm...."
(Continuing to read poem - a must read)

MIGUNA MIGUNA: Anyway, that is my scratching toe. And in the morning we had several presentations of different people. And Munyonzwe spoke, Norbese-Philip spoke, Afua Cooper spoke, Kike Roach spoke, and Charles Roach. And from what they said, there are several things that came up, you know, throughout different deliberations. Deliberations or deliberation? The English language is a tricky game.

They came up with different suggestions. And I noted some of them down. And maybe at the end of the discussion we may come back to some of them. But one was that we should create alternative institutions that serve our community and our interest. That is one. We should keep that in mind as we go along, because we should not repeat things which have been said.

Mr. Roach also said that we should strengthen the BADC and perhaps similar organizations because that is the only way we can create a permanent space of activists and activism for change.

I also heard people talk about creating an institution. Munyonzwe talked about creating an institution that would train journalists, lawyers, private investigators, institutions that perhaps will be informed with our consciousness and historical knowledge that will be sensitive to what our community interests are. He also mentioned that we should think seriously of having a magazine, a critical magazine, not a tabloid, not a newspaper, but a critical magazine.

There was also the mentioning of community activism as the ultimate solution to the problem. I think it was Kike who mentioned that. And she gave background information regarding the type of treatment that we have gotten from the mainstream society.

So given that, I am going to say -- I am going to add some few things to what they have said. As a writer, and as a lawyer and as an activist, and as an African, I feel that we do not have an institution that can produce our works of art, our creative works.

We need a publishing company. We have one publishing company called "Sister Vision Press". It targets, promotes and empowers writers of colour, women, female writers of colour. And I think it is a good thing. It is time to have a publishing firm that promotes both female writers who are African and male writers who are African. Right now we don't have any. And one will wonder, who will write our history books, who will write the histories of our struggles, who will write Dudley Law's history? Will we leave it for the *Toronto Star* and the *Sun*? I mean, is that where we are going to do our research to get the raw material upon which to write? I mean, where did people get the material to write Garvey? Garvey wrote a lot by himself. And people just had to go to that and get it.

Now, a lot of us don't have the time, some of us don't have the skills and the talents or the interest to do that. Some of us do. It is a challenge upon us to do that. Let's create alternative publishing company one with dedication and courage, and let's promote our creative works, let's promote our history.

That child sitting there, here, this child, when she grows up she goes to school and all she is told about herself is negativity. She might hate what she is. For us to prevent that we must have books, we must have video and other alternative representative means to make that child celebrate her heritage.

We cannot allow their attacks to veer us off from the course that we must struggle on. And I think that it is imperative upon us to ensure that not only do we prevent a holocaust from reoccurring -- because we have already gone through a history of holocausts: the middle passage, slavery, colonization, the more than economic holocaust has been there. We should make it impossible. We should create a situation which makes a holocaust impossible. We should not only say, like the Jews say, "Never Again". It should be impossible for anybody even to utter "Never Again". There is no way that we are going to do that if we don't write, if we don't act in theatre positively, if we don't use video and film positively, if we don't do our cultural work, if we don't raise consciousness. Nothing can come out of an empty tin without anything inside.

The basis of liberation is cultural and mental liberation. It's not the dollar; it's not a structure like this. Once you have the mind everything follows.

They say, and this is perhaps a juggle now, that the pen is mightier than the sword. Actually, to a large extent that is exactly the case.

When you attack these people very incessantly, using your own forums, they will squirm and they will run. And these people are very capable of running and hiding. How long did it take them before we remove them from the coast of Africa. And, you know, we were not that well organized. We squabbled amongst ourselves, and we kill each other a lot, but they still run. So what make you think that they cannot run from these shores of the Mississauga? They will run. And it is that challenge that I put before us today. Let's create those forums, let's create those institutions. And it needs commitment, it needs courage, it needs time, it needs patience. But we should do that.

On that note I will give this chance to Otis Richmond to say his piece, and then Colin Browne. Finally we will go to the domain of our struggles in the city, and that is Mr. Dudley Laws.

NORMAN OTIS RICHMOND: First of all, I would like to thank the organizers of this meeting. I am glad to be invited. I want to open up with a question. Who saw the *Toronto Star* yesterday? The *Toronto Star* has a story in there about a Cuban brother who defected from the basketball team.

AUDIENCE: (Answering yes, yes)

NORMAN OTIS RICHMOND: Did you see the Sun? There was a similar story. Anyway, this brother, a basketball player, defected from Cuba.

Now, the *Globe & Mail* reported that this is a police officer who talked to this brother from Cuba who defected. He said he didn't defect, he is seeking refugee status. Since Canada has diplomatic relations with Cuba, he is asking for refugee status so he is not really defecting. This is a quote from a staff sergeant. We received some information that led us to the Toronto Star. Originally the player had called the Toronto Sun for assistance and left the message on a machine for a reporter, the officer said. He didn't return the call soon enough and in the meantime the player went to the Toronto Star.

So this particular Cuban brother, I am going to give him the benefit of the doubt. I think that he has probably got bad information in terms of -- he doesn't know the history of this city.
This is a time when African people and other people of colour are calling for a boycott of the Sun. And here you have a brother coming from Cuba who runs to the Sun, the paper that we condemn, for help.

Now, I don't want to stay on this too long but, you know, the *Star*, the *Sun* nor the *Globe* never talks about the accomplishments of the Cuban revolution, but if someone defects that's big news. I mean, they should have put me on the front page of the Toronto Star when I defected from the United States. I mean, I came up here because I refused to fight in Viet Nam, but they didn't put me on the front page.

There is Assata Shakur, she is in Cuba now, why don't they put her on the front page of the Star and talk about what she is doing in Cuba today. But I just wanted to start out with that.

I want to give a bit of history about the media. On this particular continent in North America, you have three newspapers that have had an impact on people in terms of circulation. And when I talk about "circulation" I am talking about paid circulation, not when you can just go on a street corner and pick up a newspaper like you can now, not the *Star,* the *Sun* or the *Globe.* But I mean, our community papers are free. That has not always been the case. The Black Panther newspaper, the *Mohammed Speaks* newspaper and the *Negro World.*

Now, all of these papers were tied to political organizations. The Black Panther newspaper was the organ of the Black Panther party. The *Mohammed Speaks* was the organ of the Nation of Islam, and the *Negro World* was the organ of the Universal Negro Improvement Association and African Community Leagues. And Dudley and the guys changed the name to the Universal African Improvement Association. But during Garvey's time it was U.N.I.A.

The interesting thing about these particular papers was that they all -- people paid for these papers, fifty cents, or twenty-five cents. Probably twenty-five cents, I think, they used to cost. That was in the early sixties.

I would like to start with *The Negro World*, Garvey's paper. The significant thing about it was that it had a paid circulation, and it also was published in English, French and Spanish. I don't think any of our publications have done that since then. There was also a daily for it. They had a daily paper called the Negro Times for three years.

In Kenya there were accounts of people in Kenya reading this paper, bringing this paper in, people reading this paper in English, and people going into the bush, going into the interior of Kenya relating what was taking place with African people around the world.

Mohammed Speaks newspaper was the voice of the Nation of Islam. And it's very significant that we realize that *Mohammed Speaks* was the voice of the Nation of Islam. But the editors and the people that put it together were Black socialists. This is a fact.

- DR. MUNYONZWE HAMALENGWA

Elijah Mohammed wrote a column called "How to Eat to Live", and then he go do his thing. But if you read the Mohammed Speaks newspaper there was always information in there about a man who influenced me a lot, was a guy named Charles P. Howard. He had a syndicated column and he wrote a lot about Africa. He wrote a lot about Algeria. He wanted us to know what was taking place with the Ben Bella, what was taking place in Kenya, all over the African world. He read Charles Howard. But not only the African world they covered, they covered Cuba. They supported the Cuban revolution. They supported the Chinese revolution. They reported what was taking place with Korea.

We as African people in this part of the world, we knew what was taking place, we knew about Chou En Lai and Mao Tse Tung, Ho Chi Minh in Vietnam, we knew about Kim IL Sung in Korea. I mean, we were not any political illiterate people. This was because of the things that we read in the *Mohammed Speaks* newspaper.

The Black Panther newspaper came out after that. And, you know, the Black Panther newspaper came in the sixties. And they had such writers as Huey Newton, Elaine Brown, George Jackson who we are going to mention. George Jackson used to write a column in there. And near the end of -- I guess around the middle time of their tenure they brought in from Egypt, Dubois' son, David Dubois, who was Dubois' son. They brought him from Egypt and he became the editor of the Black Panther paper. Once again, we had information about all the liberation movements that were taking place in Africa, we knew about Guinea Bissau, we knew about Amilcar Cabral, we knew about the PAC, we knew about FRELIMO, we knew about the MPLA, we knew about who Jonas Savimbi was, we knew that he was a traitor; we knew about him way back there.

So we are saying that these particular papers existed then. And Al Hamilton, who just passed away, published *Contrast* in 1969. He was under the influence of all of this action that was taking place with these publications here, as well as his own life experience.

Now, some of the newspapers that existed then, coming out of North America, you had papers like *Bucklow Challenger*. You had the kit from Jackson, Mississippi, which is still going on, the *Chicago Defenders*. And I submit today that the Black press in Toronto is not challenging, defending or advocating anything by and large. And it's for free. You can't sell a publication here anymore because it's -- somebody went along and started giving these newspapers away.

So today we have a "*Burning Spear*". Has anybody ever seen a *Burning Spear*?
(No reply)

Okay. We have a *Burning Spear* that is coming out. The Black Panther paper had an issue just the other day about Black homelessness. And we have the *Final Call*. The *Final Call*, you can get it on the streets of Toronto. The Panther paper is hard to come by and the *Burning Spear* is hard to come by. We don't have that particular press.

I submit today that we need not only a newspaper, we need a newspaper that's tied to a political movement. That is the difference between what took place yesterday and what's taking place today.

If BADC is the organization there needs to be a publication coming from BADC, or any organization that's a vanguard organization needs a political organ, a newspaper. That's one thing we can thing about. And Cleveland Moulton, who is in the audience today, who is a member of BADC, used to put together *Contrast* in the old days.

Okay. Besides the newspaper I think there is another initiative that I think people need to know about. And that is the Milestone initiative which is headed by a group of predominantly Black business people, Denham Jolly, Jean Augustine, I think people like that have a lot to do with that.

Now, a radio station -- I am a music person. But I really don't want to talk about music, because I think that if we have a radio station the most important part of the radio station is not necessarily the music. Just as important as the music that would pay our artists and so on and so forth is the spoken word.

We need two radio stations, one which would deal with the spoken word and one which would deal with music. And we would have to have some sixty/forty, with forty percent talk and sixty percent music, or thirty percent talk, or some sort of breakdown, but we need a talk format so we can communicate. We need a forum so we can communicate with one another.

The only talk show that we have right now on a consistent basis is one o'clock in the morning, Doctor Love. It comes on on CHIN on a Wednesday night. And I don't know nobody -- you can't deal with that.

- DR. MUNYONZWE HAMALENGWA

Christie Blatchford can run her stuff in the *Sun* and on CFRB-1010, and give her same commentary over the radio. Milton Blake cannot do that. He can do a free show on CKLN, and he can't sell his commentary anywhere. If we had a radio station and it was accountable to us, I would suggest that a person like Milton Black should get paid for his radio show and get paid for his commentary, which we -- and I am including everybody in this room, I don't care what colour you are -- would benefit from commentaries by Milton Blake. Because I think that it's important that we as African people we have something to say, we as Asian people, I think we have something to say. I don't think that the leadership of the world is coming from Europe anymore. That's just my view of it. I think the thinkers are coming from Africa, Asia, Latin America. That's where the brain power is today.

Cable television. I do a cable TV show. And that's a dangerous thing in the sense that it is a freebie. And I don't think that we should be doing things we don't get paid for, but this is a training ground. While I think that we should think of cable TV is easy to get on if you have an idea, you don't get paid. We have to figure out some sort of way to get paid for our creations, and where we own these things. [Tape interrupted and not transcribed]

COLIN BROWNE:

... I have got some handouts. I will ask you just to take one and pass it down.

All right. What we just heard was -- this is just an article that says at the bottom, in the third column there -- you don't have to read it all now, but at the bottom, in the third column there:
"The average American murder victim is a 12 to 15-year-old Black boy."

The point is that there is a gender specific nature to the problem that we have been talking about.

With respect to the question of picket signs and non-picket signs, we definitely have to have both going on.

I practice criminal law, and one of the problems I have is with the cross-examination of police during a police case, and with the judges directing juries basically to convict when the accused is Black and all this kind of stuff. And it is very difficult to get all that on a placard and go and picket. These are very complicated issues that need a little bit more -- you got to be basically sitting down at a table to discuss them. But that's not to give the picketers a hard time. We need everything. That's how people work.

There was a lady earlier who made a comment about her purse being made of scraps. What we have to understand as a community is that in order to run an organization, especially a business, in order to sort of gain economic empowerment, we have to do what the African who is putting those purses together is doing. We can't waste anything. As she said, we can't waste people. And she made a particular comment. She said, no matter how middle class somebody looks, they may be useful. The point being that we need the lower, middle, upper and basically everybody has to get down and pitch in and do what it is they do best.

I am middle class. I came from Nova Scotia, my parents were wealthy. I was the only Black in a white wealthy neighbourhood. And they later moved to Jamaica where in fact they are still wealthy. And we moved down there. They are from Antigua and Trinidad. And I have been in Toronto now for five years practicing law. So I have got a fairly broad-based exposure to some different Black populations. And the problems are the same.

In Nova Scotia we have been doing this kind of thing forever. My mother was doing the same kind of thing. As one other lady said earlier, it's not a new problem we have got, but it is worthwhile to come together and discuss new angles. And Munyonzwe suggested, well, threatened that we should be able to produce some new suggestions here today. So that's what I am going to do. So he basically said, you don't have to be concerned about making friends here. And I am generally not concerned about making friends so I may not go over all that well with somebody. And that's too bad.

As I walked out of here to get something to drink about 20 minutes ago, I was standing across the street and a white guy comes up to me and he says, you are lawyer, aren't you? And I said, yeh. And I said, with the hair it's not difficult to pick me out so this happens all the time. So I said to him, yes, that's right. He said, well, I have got a trial on November such and such and I don't have a lawyer and I have got a problem, can you represent me. So I said, fine, what's the story. And he said, well, such and such a cop planted narcotics on me, and bla, bla, bla, I didn't have a thing, and he said that he found such and such in his pants. It's a white guy. And all the criminal lawyers here, all the people who are not closely connected to the justice system are going to be hearing this story from Blacks, whites, men, women, everybody under the sun all the time. Somebody is lying here. The police always say they didn't do it, okay. So there is something bad going on here. And we can't just pick a Queen's block and say, police stop lying. I mean, you have to develop a more sophisticated strategy.

Now, there is a more sophisticated strategy that's being produced now. And I won't point them out, but the person who is doing it is in the room presently. And he has got a data base on corrupt police behaviour that is quite sophisticated. And we as a Black community need to barter for him whether he is Black, white, female or hermaphrodite. We need to offer him, her, them, all the support we can because that's what we need. Okay? We need to be able to trace police of state behaviour, so that when we get to court, when me and the criminal lawyers get to court we have something more than just police inconsistent statements to go with. Right now we show how the police, well, he said this at the preliminary inquiry, you said this here and you said something else there, but the jury still think that the police officer was probably tired on this day and a little bit confused on the next day and maybe had a fight with his wife the next day. It's biased towards conflicting statements, because the jury have this fear of the police or, I don't know if you call it respect for the state. If there is a psychologist in here maybe they can explain what it is. But for some reason there is a bias towards conviction. If you combine with the judges who are representing our community, they are all white males. Not all of them, but definitely most of them. They have, in my opinion, instructed the jury basically to convict. Their instructions to the jury are sometimes so sophisticated I can't understand. The lawyers always have to ask the judge to explain the charge to the jury. So if the lawyers have to ask the judge what he has just said, the jury is more confused by a long shot.

So the jury will listen to this huge amount of legal wrangling and then go into the jury room. And the only thing I believe that they are going to remember, is that the judge said "You have to be sure the guy is guilty". That's what it boils down to. So that's nothing. That's simply nothing.

Anyway, what I am suggesting is that we put together an organization -- which I will get into a little bit more shortly and then a little more in depth. Put together an organization which has interest in helping those who are compiling data bases. We have to get on computer to track police lying and other inappropriate behaviour. And we have to do that quickly.

Now, in order to do this we have to put together a group that is a permanent thing, it's not going to last for six months or a year, it's got to be on-going and it is to start now and it's going to last forever, or until the problem goes away, whichever comes first.

Then the group has to have a lot of people, it has to have a lot of energy, it has to have a lot of resources, it has to have a lot of passion, it has to have a lot of anger, and it's probably not going to readily get a lot of money from Bob Rae. Okay? It's probably going to get money from private sources, most likely itself. So we have to have a group that is capable of actually earning in the free market.

Now, Black people have been earning in the free market for a long time, so we ought to be able to handle that.

Let me give you a little bit more. First, let me just read something. Play a little game and you can tell me what the following passage is:

"When in the course of human events it becomes

necessary for one people to dissolve the political bonds which have connected them with one another, and to assume among the powers of the earth the separate and equal station to which the laws of nature and the nature's God entitled them, a decent respect for the opinions of mankind requires that they should declare the causes which impel them to the separation. We hold these truths to be self-evident, that all men are created equal, that they are endowed by their creator with certain inalienable rights, that among these are life, liberty and the pursuit of happiness, that to secure these rights governments are instituted among men deriving their just powers from the consent of the government, that whenever any form of government becomes destructive of these ends it is the right of the people to alter or to abolish it and to institute new government laying its foundation on such principles and organizing its powers in such form as to them shall seem most likely to affect their safety and happiness. Prudence indeed will dictate that governments long established should not be changed for light and transient causes. And accordingly all experiences have shown that mankind are more disposed to suffer while evils are sufferable than to right themselves by abolishing the forms to which they are accustomed. But when a long trail of abuses and usurpations pursuing invariably the same object ... and design to reduce them under absolute despotism, it is their right, it is their duty to throw off such government and to provide new guards for their future security. Such has been the patient sufferance of these colonies, and such is now the necessity which constrains them to alter their former systems of government.

The history of the present King of Great Britain is a history of repeated injury and usurpations, all having indirect object the establishment of absolute tyranny over these states. To prove this let the facts be submitted to a candid world."

Now, that's the Declaration of Independence of the United States. This is much less political.

Everybody here almost has something from a newspaper here in Toronto. And I have something you probably all saw in the *Toronto Sun*, July 3rd, "Jamaica No Problem", a five-page special report on Jamaica. I don't know if anybody saw this. But needless to say, it's got the little Black boys, little angelic Black boys, and it goes on basically to say, we really got a problem because all these criminals are coming to Canada.

There is a quote from some guy painting here of wooden birds in Ochio Rios, who says:

"If I were in charge I would do the same as the cops, kill the bad guys so they don't kill you."

Well, it's very, very popular nowadays for white people to quote Black people who say stupid things. That's very, very common. But I don't have to go into the detail of what's happening here in Metro Toronto with the Jamaican population. In Nova Scotia I was involved in the Marshall Inquiry, which was an inquiry into the justice system, where a Native Indian wound up spending twelve years of age. And in Sidney, Cape Breton an investigation was done. It was so pathetic that they decided to hold an inquiry and look into what exactly was going on.

I was working with the Black United Front, because the guy who actually died in this whole equation, which not everybody realizes was Black. This is a guy who wound up disemboweled and bled to death. And we suggested that, you know, the fact that it was a Black guy who was disemboweled and bled to death probably slowed down the investigation a little further.

Here now -- that's the situation we are dealing with in Nova Scotia. Not all that many West Indians, it was an indigenous Black population and indigenous Native population and an old world white establishment. Here it's a little different. But here instead of nigger you got Jamaican. And there was the nigger down and now you hear Jamaican, it's the same thing.

What they have suggested in the *Toronto Sun* is that what has happened is the Black people who basically run around having sex anyway, and they don't stay in nice nuclear family units, they have a sort of a tribalish -- tribalesque extended family back in the tropics, and when they come up here they have a hard time adjusting to our nice little white nuclear family so they go around shooting police officers. That is a scary oversimplification of what's going on.

The racism in Canada is being sort of -- you use the term white wash, people are suggesting that really there is no racism in Canada, that really if the Black would behave everything would be okay. I was born here and white anti-Black racism as we all know here is alive and well and is not a function of dysfunctional negro families. That's not what's going on there.

Now, I am getting a bit off topic. Because the point is the Black men's leadership association is simply a call to alms for the Black male who is the primary recipient of bullets to the head to stand up and take control of our situation.

I will hand out copies of this. I will finish with a song that I wrote in honour of this occasion. And it's called "Pay Back Owed to Big White Sister":
"I came up here in 1989 and I very hoped that I would find enlightened thinkers and active groups, not fools jumping through hoops. Much to my surprise and sorrow, I met a herd of sheep, a hound of wining weasels wandering blindly headed for sleep. A few good men, a few good women, but mostly hum-drum clowns. But now it's time to turn the tide and make unpleasant. Someone here is lying while all the brothers are dying, and we may never know the whole bloody story. However, I have come to tell you we must reclaim our lost former glory. Our warriors must now assemble, we must outfit and train our troops. We must neutralize big, bad, white sister and hang her with her own hoops."
Thank you.

MIGUNA MIGUNA: We will now hear what Dudley Laws has to say.

DUDLEY LAWS: What should I say. Well, first of all, I am very honoured this evening to be a part of this panel. And I will try to put some input into this discussion.

As Black people living in this country it is still my opinion that we are being subjected to the harshest kinds of treatment than any other group in this society. And as I look retrospectively at the problems that we have been having over the years, I see an increase of the confrontation, racist confrontation between government institutions such as the police, immigration, and other agencies against our people.

And I must remind you that some of us within our own community seem to forget some of the problems that are confronting us as a people.
Let us look at the police problem, first of all. Just 1978 when we had the killing of Buddy Evans in the Flying Disco, and the demonstrations that ensued after that, the protestations for charges to be laid against the police officers that murdered Buddy Evans. We saw that no charge was laid in that case. But the shootings continued. The killing of our young men continued. The brutalization of our women, the insults on us as African people continue.

After Buddy Evans -- and I just want to remind you, because some of us who are recent in Toronto do not know the history of police hostilities. And we find people calling meetings and organizing discussion with police to talk about the problems when they know nothing about the problems.

After Buddy Evans we had the problems of -- the murdering of Albert Johnson by the police. Albert Johnson was shot to death kneeling down, according to his then seven-year-old daughter, Colsey. Shot to death, murdered in his own home. The Black community went out and demonstrated, demanded that charges be laid against the police officers. Of course, charges were eventually laid.

The Police officers were acquitted by a white jury, white judge, white prosecutor. And after several years of demonstrating for justice in the Albert Johnson case, the courts finally gave an award to Mrs. Johnson of some three hundred thousand dollars. But in giving the award they said, we are not taking liability for this death. And so they settled the Johnson killing.

Now, between 1979 to about 1988 there had been numerous confrontations with police. We saw the Jamestown incident where hundreds of police officers converged on Jamestown, going into people's homes without warrants, arresting people, strip-searching people on the grounds of Jamestown.

Jamestown is a housing complex at Kipling and Finch, mostly occupied by people of African descent.

And in that incident one young lady stated that her six-month-old child was thrown across the room by police officers. We had demonstrations, we went to Queen's Park. We were involved in a lot of actions around that incident. But nobody was ever made to give an account for the incidents at Jamestown. No one was ever held accountable. And so we go on, and then we have in 1988, I think, the shooting of Lester Donaldson. Lester Donaldson was shot three months before he was fatally shot again by the Metropolitan Police Force.

Police said they had a call that Lester Donaldson had hostages. When they arrived Lester was on his own, having his supper, sitting at the side of his bed. And this was from the new release given by Chief Marks at the time.

When they went in they said to Donaldson, Lester, we want to speak to you. He said, I don't want to speak to you guys. By this time Lester could hardly walk. He was seen on Eglington the previous day on crutches, you know, dragging his leg along the road. Five police officers were in the room with Lester Donaldson, including one of the officers that was responsible for shooting Lester previously.

Lester Donaldson had in his hand a small peering knife that he was using to help him eat his food. And I was at the preliminary hearing, and when the knife was introduced the judge had to bend forward to see the knife. That's how small the knife was. And they said that Lester lounged at them with this peering knife and they shot him to defend police officers, the five police officers. And they shot him to death: five police officers, five guns, five truncheons. And it was revealed at the trial that the police called the ambulance before they shot Lester Donaldson, and the Emergency Task Force before they shot him. And they said they were speaking about Lester the evening before, they knew him well. They shot Lester Donaldson to death.

So when people want to meet with police and talk to police and do not know the history of police actions in Toronto, and in Canada for that matter, they should educate themselves around police issues before.

- DR. MUNYONZWE HAMALENGWA

And then the shooting of Michael Wade Lawson. Some young fellow stole a car from a garage one evening. Police knew who they were. They knew some of the parents. They saw the car. They knew where the car was going. And they waited for the car to go to Michael Wade Lawson's aunt's home to drop off his cousin. They waited for the car.

One officer removed the normal bullet from his gun and replaced it with the Dum-Dum bullet that explodes on impact. And as the car drove up, Dale came out of the car, the cousin of Wade Lawson, the car backed out of the driveway. The police say that they were in front of the car, but yet the bullet entered through the back of the car and struck Michael Wade Lawson in the back of his head.

And when you sat in the courtroom, which I did, during the preliminary hearing and the trial, you could not help but feel -- not only hear but feel the lies that came out in these hearings and trials. At the end of the preliminary hearing Judge Draper, who is now deceased after the trial, increased the charges to second degree murder. Yet the officers were acquitted by yet another white jury, white judge, white prosecutor. And it continues.

The shooting of Sophia Cook, who sat in the front passenger seat of a car with her seatbelt on posing no danger to the police officer, shot in the centre of her back. The officer said, Oh, it was a mistake, it was an accident.

When this trial went to court the judge said, Oh, he was only charged with the careless handling of a firearm anyway, no mention of any injury to anybody. The judge said, Oh, the officers rights were violated, so he threw the charges out.

I think the Province of Ontario appealed and then the officer went back to court and was again acquitted.

And then we have Marlon Neil, who ran a radio trap, but eventually stopped. In court this Italian gave witness and she said, "I saw the police officer walking around the car with his gun drawn while Marlon Neil was sitting in the car with the door locked." She said, "The officer fired one shot in the ground then two shots in the body of the car", striking Marlon Neil in the back.

The Black community was upset once again, as we always are, demonstrated. The officer was charged.

In charging the jury this was a part of the comments of the judge, "What do you want, do you want the officer to take his hands and stop the car?" I mean, this was the judge. He said if the officer wanted to kill Marlon Neil he had three more bullets left in his gun. That was the judge. And the officer was acquitted. I think he was the one who became the chauffeur for McCormack or one of those people.

And we have the shooting of a Black youth that was shot. It was never disclosed what his name was. And he was shot by a Black officer who was chasing some young people around and eventually shot them.

And then you have the shooting of Jonathan Howard.

Then we have Rohan Boglaw. This is a young fellow who was shot on Wellesley, I think. Some lady stated, Oh, yes, I was attacked by some young men, three young Black men. And this police officer, the first set of Black youth he saw he went crazy. He pulled his gun and he started firing, like the Wild West, striking Rohan Boglaw in the back twice, then turned around and charged him for robbery. And this was somebody who allegedly attempted to steal her purse, and yet they charged him for robbery. And the charges were thrown out of court.

And it goes on again. We have Raymond Lawrence at Lansdowne and Bloor, shot under very questionable circumstances by police. They ran him down, jumping several fences as he tried to get away from them. They shot him while attempting to flee for his life. They shot him anyway, claiming he had a knife. There was so many conflicting evidence about that knife. But they got away with that too.

Then we have the shooting of Ian Coley. Police stopped the car for no obvious reason. He said he saw Ian Coley with a gun. And this came out the other day when the SIU decided not to charge the officer. The officer said Ian Coley fired a shot at him. But when the SIU did their investigation -- and some of you must have read this -- the gun was not fired at all; the gun that was supposed to be Ian Coley's gun was not fired. And the strangest part of all this investigation was that the officer who went to the scene of the shooting said he saw the officer who shot Ian Coley with two guns in his hand, his service revolver and the gun that was supposed to be Ian Coley's gun. He said he took the service revolver -- this belongs to the officer -- from him but let him retain the gun that was supposed to be Ian Coley's, which he went into the cruiser and he took it to 42 Division with him. And the SIU said, we cannot understand how this could ever be. Now, when they test the gun they found that the gun had never been fired at all. And they do not see that. And this is the kind of thing that is happening within our police force. And that is why we find nowadays people Like Mr. McCormack and Mr. Lymer want to be around to discipline Black people. They have good pensions, they want to be here. I mean, they think they have a responsibility to be around in Toronto so they can say time and time again that Black people commit a disproportionate amount of crime. And I am telling you that we as Black people, African people that live in this City of Toronto have to begin to understand what we are up against. We are at war with the police force and with the criminal justice system, and we must deal with that.

And then we have the police working with the Immigration Department. The other day the Minister of Immigration met secretly with the police force of Metropolitan Toronto and created a task force to deal with illegal immigrants. Why? Because they are shooting up police officers and the Just Desert incident, as if people who commit crimes only come from the Caribbean and only are Black.

I read about a gentleman from Europe who killed his wife, burnt her, crushed the charred body and sprinkled it in his garden, and he is supposed to be getting citizenship in a couple of weeks. And I don't hear Christie Blatchford or Worthington or anybody saying anything. His deportation order was removed. I haven't heard any of these racist columnists speaking about this incident. But as soon as a Black youth does shoplifting or have a problem in school, the pictures appear in the Toronto Sun and on television.

They talk about deportation, and I hear a so-called adjudicator who is saying he is sorry that he gave a release hearing to some of these people who supposed to have committed crime. There is a process, and nobody explains the immigration process. It seems like everybody is taking the responsibility or blame because a Black person is involved. In the process of immigration, the last process rests with the Immigration Appeal Board. And even if an adjudicator gives a release to a person who is in violation of the Immigration Act, the Immigration Appeal Board makes the final decision and then removal takes place. And who is responsible when the Immigration Department takes a long time to make such a decision. It is not the fault of the person who is concerned in these matters.

So we find that the attack on our community extend itself even to the education system. Now you have within the education system the "zero tolerance", where two young people get into a confrontation and they have a fight or a knife is drawn or something, you deprive that person or want to deprive that individual of an education, which makes that person become unemployable, that person will not have gainful employment, then that person will likely get involved in criminal activities and they go into the criminal justice eventually and be incarcerated. So from the early stages of our lives as Black people we have a problem. And that problem has been so pronounced in our communities over the years that we all have a responsibility to do something about it. It is very, very important.

I am very angry many times when I see some of the things that are happening. A gentleman came into my office a couple weeks ago. And let me refresh my memory of this person's name. He came into my office, and he says to me, I am setting up a meeting with Mr. Lymer and Mr. McCormack. And he said, Alan Tonks might be there too. And this person is somebody called Derrick Morris, right. You must have seen him on television. He said to me, I am setting up this meeting, and it is important, Mr. Laws, that you come to this meeting. So I sat and I looked at him, and I couldn't really believe what he was saying. And he continued and he said, the reason why I think you should come, he says, I think I have the answers, I think I have the answer to the problems between the Black community and the police. I said, the Black Action Defence Committee has taken a position that we will not speak to police until they publicly admit that there is a problem within the police force, and I have no intention of going. He insisted. You should come, he said. You know, he said, you can come and you can say to them that you are sorry for all what you have done. At this point I was looking around for a baseball bat. I simply said to him, you know, I can't deal with this. I said, you know, I have work to do, I think you had better leave. Well, I was surprised when I was sitting at home last Sunday night and this man appears on television and saying some nonsense, you know. He want to make white people richer? He didn't say that on television, you know, but when I read the report in Share and some of the things that this fellow was saying I laughed. And then I got so emotional. And then I said to myself, in 1994, if we can have Black people, or a Black person saying things like this, you know. I mean, he is talking about civilization. He said white people have civilized the world and have given technology to the world and we Black people can't take it from them. We never said we wanted to take anything from anybody. I mean, if I called this man an idiot, I mean, I would be justified, but I will not call him an idiot. I don't know what to call him. It is a very sad situation, when we have young people who are depending on us as mature individuals, expecting that we should give them guidance and we have someone like this who would come to undermine and to destroy some of the progressive work that many of us have done in this community. I think it is very sad. We say that we want to organize different things to deal with problems in our community.

our brothers, and some of our sisters also, when it is close to winter time and the lake is beginning to freeze, and baptize them, you know, seriously. You know, I can deal with Mr. McCormack, because we have been dealing with them, we have, and we have made a great impact on them. Sometimes we can ignore them, you know, just pass them by and do what we have to do. But when a brother or sister within our community begin to mess up and do things like this, sometimes we do not know what to do with them. If we knew their mothers we could call their mothers and say, look, your son and daughter is doing something bad. But seriously, we have to begin to address these issues. Because Mr. Lymer sits there and says Blacks make up a disproportionate number of criminals in the society, after this guy spoke. He has not convinced Mr. Lymer that there is criminality in all of society and all of the communities regardless of where the community lives. We have a serious problem in our community besides the police. And there is young people killing each other. And we have to address that too. We cannot always talk about, the man is wrong, the man is shooting us. Of course they are. And we have to deal with that problem as well. But we have problems within our community that must be dealt with. We have been going around to the schools, the universities and speaking to young people, and we have to do that. I have no intention of going on television or the newspaper to say our young people are criminals and they are bad. I was bad when I was growing up as a child in school, I got into fights. Nobody called the police when I was going to school to arrest me or arrest the person I was fighting with. Those of us who came from the Caribbean and those of us who have been here in earlier years in Canada had a chance of a good education. Whether we accept it or not, we had. Why should we now deprive our young people of that, which is so necessary for them to be guided by their experiences and knowledge that they have obtained through the educational process. Why should they be deprived? We have to encourage our young people. We have to lift them up. Because the few that are in society, in our community that are causing the problem seems to overshadow the brilliance of many of our young people that are striving for excellence. So it grieves me when someone such as Derrick Morris, or Lincoln Alexander, for that matter, comes out and talk nonsense because they want to be associated with others whom they believe better than themselves. Those are not the kinds of examples that we must set as Black people.

One of the suggestions that I have, I think we must begin to establish cells, small groups of people within this community, in the Ontario Housing complex, in all the communities. Even if it's five, or four or ten people getting together every day to talk about internal problems where they live, and to link it with bigger organizations.

The next suggestion, complaints must be -- all complaints against the police, complaints in the educational system, complaints in the housing complex must be documented by us. We must have a plank of information that we can use. It must be compiled. Every Monday morning when we go back to the Black Action Defence Committee, the amount of telephone calls about police, confrontation with police, Ontario Housing, people who have been arrested, no bail for young people in detention centres. No. We have a problem. And because of the fights that we have put up over the years against racism, we saw the establishment of the Special Investigation Unit which, in my opinion, is a valuable unit in the society today, which benefits not only Black people but everybody. But it needs to be strengthened. We need to give the unit support and make sure that it is not disbanded by any government, whether the government is NDP, the Liberals or the Conservative.

We have seen the establishment of the Police Complaints Commission. That needs a lot of restructuring. That also must be supported by us. We cannot sit down and only come together when there is a time of crisis. Our work must be continuous. Like the immortal Garvey said -- and I always like to quote my mentors -- he says, "Chance has never yet satisfied the hope of the suffering people". He said it is action, self-reliance and the vision of self that has been the only means by which the oppressed has seen and realized the hope of their own freedom. And I believe that all of us have that responsibility to give courage and guidance to our young people, and to ourselves. Because some of us may be looking matured, but some of us, like this young man here, the green of infancy, you know, not yet developed to understand where we now stand in the history of this time. Because as we look at the stages of our progress as a people, and on that road that lead us to where we are now, we saw people like Malcolm, Garvey, Nkruma, and Nanny, Martin Luther King, and a lot of local people in this City of Toronto, who have helped to build this society, where we can get some semblance of respect and semblance of justice. And that must be maintained. As for myself and the problems that I am confronting, I am glad for the support that the community has given, and that it has been solid support. Lawyers such as Charlie Roach, Peter Rosenthal, and many others have stood by. And sometimes when I listen to the evidence against me in court I smile to myself, because you know when somebody got up on the stand and said, oh, Dudley Laws agreed to change a million in coins to dollar bills, you know, and nonsense like that, and other things that is ludicrous, you know.

I know the purpose of my travelling, but that will not work. I am like a tiger that is entrapped. I will fight harder to get out of that entrapment. (Applause)

So I think it is a good way of getting together. I think this gathering, you know, will come up with some solutions that will help us to carry on the fight to get us out of this problem. Because none of us want to see another person get shot, whether that person is black or white. And talking about that, look at Sabatino Norvego. I mean Sabatino was an Italian shot by the police. The brother there and he said to the police officer, don't shoot my brother, he is not well. The police put two bullets in his chest, when he could have just eased off and let the young man cool down.

So it is a police force that we are dealing with, with men who are now jostling for power to continue their oppression against us. They want to be there.

But even when I talk about Mr. McCormack leaving, the big question is, will any other one of them be any different to us whether he remains or go? That is the question, and a very important question. Are we going to be bothered about who will take the reins of restructuring the police force, from Mr. McCormack. I wouldn't waste any time on that myself. I would rather work within my community to deal with the problems in my communities, because I am not convinced that the one who will take over from him will be any better than he is. So I don't think we should worry about who takes over from McCormack or whether Art Lymer should get an extension of his retirement or not. As far as I am concerned he has been retired a long time.

So, Brothers and Sisters, we must continue the fight to extricate ourselves from this oppressive and racist society. We must. And I will play my part as I usually do, without hesitation or compromise. Thank you very much.

MIGUNA MIGUNA: Thank you very much. I would like to thank all the panelists, both the panelists in the morning and the ones who have just concluded deliberations now. And I would also like to thank the audience for their rapt attention, and their participation in the morning particularly. And hopefully we are going to have a lively discussion.

I just wanted to mention in passing that this week's *Share* has some very interesting things in it. First of all, there is this written plan, which I actually saw in the *Toronto Star.* The European Heritage Week, which is supposed to be taking place October 9th to 15th, it's been, according to this report, it has been endorsed by the Queen herself, the Queen of England, your great Queen, and by mayors of Halifax and Victoria.

Now, it's not a matter of reacting, but I think we need to make a statement. And this statement should be an organized statement; it should not be incremental individuals making statements here and there to the press. We need to think carefully on how we are going to respond to that. And perhaps this might be a catalyst of such, you know, a brain storm, or the response. Then, of course, there is that juvenile of theatrics, which I saw. He is supposed to be the director of "negroid affairs". They have negroid, caucasian and mongoloid affairs. So he is the director of negroid affairs. And my brother Dudley Laws mentioned -- I will quote some of the things he has said for those who have not seen it:

"We can never take the world from 'you whites'", he said. "You have done a lot of good and you have given us technological innovations and societal strategies." Right? "I don't think the police would violate a person's human rights just like that. I don't look like a criminal." So he thinks that because he assists himself not to look like a criminal, as far as I am concerned he is a criminal as I am.

And then on August 9th the *Globe & Mail* had an editorial by the side called, "Why Africa ignores it's tragedies." And I will read the first paragraph, because I think it is important for us to notice what they are saying about us too.

"If it takes the spectacle of open mass graves and children sobbing over their dead mothers to create international interest in Africa, that is not so difficult to understand. Africans are far away."
But how to explain Africa's indifference to itself", the editorialist asks:

"For however inadequate critics may consider the White House airlift or the French peacekeeping missions called in after genocidal explosion, these are acts of .... compassion compared to what Africans themselves have done in this and that and other tragedies."
Now, that is what that says. There has also been a report compiled by the Department of Statistics Canada or Revenue Canada, which states that as recent -- I think it's is based on statistics of 1991. And this most people have heard.

"The census data show that immigrants, meaning those who would have been landed immigrants as well as successful refugee claimants, are better educated and more likely to be in the labour force than people born here in Canada."

But what does one of the cultural commentaries in Canada say? This guy is called Michael Coren. He immigrated here recently from Britain, but of course just absorbed into the mainstream right away. He says about a conference that was supposed to be only for the people of colour, he excludes -- like, white people are not supposed to attend, according to them. He says:
"These people have not needed any advice or help in rioting in the past. And this is surely another example of whites interfering in matters of colour and attempting to impose liberal imperialism on a people who evidently need it not. Stop the white man's funding, I say, By any means necessary."

Now, many things come to mind when I look at those things: one, they are procreation of our voices, and ridicule of our struggles. And then, third, is the fact that even though the predators have caused our condition, you know, the vultures do not come to a carcass which is still alive, it only comes to a carcass which is dead. They caused our death, then they eat our carcass, then they turn around and they say, look how stinky and smelly you are, you know, stinky and smelly, get up and go. Now, that is the situation we are facing. And as far as I am concerned -- it is something Norbese had mentioned -- it is a systemic, institutionalized, white supremacist system that has gone on for too long. It's over 200 years -- as a matter of fact, it is over 500 years. And we are still going through the same, same thing. How long does it take us to suffer, to die, in order to wake up from our slumber. I think it is time for us to do that.

I will read the suggestions that various panelists made in terms of what we need to do. Then we will discuss those things. And those who are interested in pursuing one, or two or three of those should leave their names, their phone numbers, and should get in touch with either me or Munyonzwe, and we can carry it forward from there. Dudley Laws is also here. He is from the Black Action Defense Committee. Get in touch with him. If you want to talk to any of the panelists you are free to do so.

One of the suggestions was to create a foundation or something that will -- as an institution will deal with our interests.

The other one was to strengthen the Black Action Defense Committee.

The third was to have a media watch, something that will cut across all things pertaining to us, how we are reported, who report what on us and how they do it, and how we can deal with it. The Jews have done that and have done that quite successfully. It is not just capitalist, it's not just money. They tediously researched and catalogued all this. And so before you touch them you panic, because you don't know what they will use that for.

The fourth is a publishing company. We should think about having one.

The fifth is a magazine, a progressive magazine. Critical.

The sixth is an institute. Legal or whatever, we can conceive and think of such.

The seventh is to perhaps to campaign and activate for the criminalization of racism. I think Kike mentioned it. And I think that is crucial. You see, it should be in the *Criminal Code* that to utter a racist word is criminal, just as much as leering at a woman or assault -- racism is so far reaching, more than any crime than we could ever mention.

The eighth is -- somebody mentioned something about alternative penitentiaries or jails. Now, personally, I have problems with not demystifying the institutions that they have already created. Perhaps we actually do need jails; perhaps we need to create other institutions through which we can reform our so-called deviants or criminals.

KIKE ROACH: I think there were alternatives mentioned, which is another means of dealing with criminal activity outside the prison.

MIGUNA MIGUNA: And Mr. Roach added that perhaps what we need is to invade the jails and teach our brothers and sisters incarcerated there, not through the mainstream institutional educational forums, but groups like us, conscious people, because people who get paid by the system are compromised by the system anyways.

There is something that I thought about but I never mentioned. We should think about radicalizing Caribana as a cultural outlet of our people. Let's not just boogieing, you know. I mean, it's good to boogey. But it's also good to boogey with the cultural ambiance, you know. It is not just good to boogey in a vacuum. When we listen to European music it says something about a specific history. It is not a vacuum, it is not just a carnival which is just about flesh. Anyway, I think that Caribana must be radicalized.

Number eleven, move towards the black-focused schools. This is the campaign we must support. Groups such as Mr. Dudley Laws' group must make statements regarding this. A push must be done very forcefully so that our children do not grow up sterile, like the permissive cultures put it. Youth clubs would help in that. There was a specific mention about our kids going to youth clubs in native communities, getting in touch with the art and things like that. These are things we should organize; we should organize trips to Africa.

[Dudley Laws (Dudley Laws continuing)]

.... You have truck drivers, you have people, riggers and buildings and, you know, these people get killed every day, electricians whose jobs are more dangerous than police officers. So when a police officer dies, nobody should glorify or be glad about it. But then, other people die every day in serious jobs. A guy coming from Florida with a truck load of oranges and crashed on the 401. Does he call ten thousand other truck drivers to come to his funeral. And we have to try and put this thing in intelligent context and look at it and say, well in five years one police officer died on the job. I mean, are they making all this noise because he was shot by a Black person, when on the highway north of Toronto an OPP officer was shot to death by a white person. And you don't hear anything about it but one day. A police officer shot another police officer in Niagara Falls. After two days in the papers it disappears. A police officer's son shot a neighbour's son with his father's gun, you don't hear anything about it.

So what I am saying is, we must not begin, you know, to get confused by all this public relations effort to indict the whole Black community.

MIGUNA MIGUNA: That sister then Munyonzwe, and then we almost come to a close. So let's have only three contributions, the sister, Munyonzwe and somebody else.

(UNIDENTIFIED SPEAKER) I think, as a person working in the court system, I think we are ignoring the problems of the youth. They are not like the youth a few years ago when they wouldn't fight back. Many of the kids I work with will tell you they are not afraid to die. If that's how the system sees them, that's how they are going to be. I know one youth, he would rob, he would steal the police officer's cars. He specifically picked out their car just to go in. And you wonder, like, what are they thinking.

Now, I know that when you guys said that we can't work together, we have to try in some way to get something to work, to get all the different communities together: I am here, you are there and another person is going to be here, but then we are not being heard unless we come to meeting like this, and there is not enough of us coming to the meetings, like community centres like Tropicana, you know, Harambee. Those people have to be here also to hear what you are saying. So we are trying to get the community together. We may not always agree on everything. We won't, because we all have our different opinions. But the way that we have to structure, the white man, they will sit there and they will not be honest, they will agree with everything that you say, but they will sit there and they will pretend. And when we get into a group together we tend to lose it with each other, we take our frustration out on each other. And we can't afford to do that. We cannot work alone, we need each other. And our kids need us, they need us.

MIGUNA MIGUNA: At the end of this if everybody could leave your names and numbers, and let's do something. Munyonzwe?

MUNYONZWE HAMALENGWA: I just want to make two points regarding what the media and the courts do to us. I just want to give two quick examples. Did you know that once it was mentioned that Clinton Gayle was shot, after a time they stopped mentioning that? Right now nobody mentions that that man was even shot. It was as if he shot a police officer and that's it, and that he was injured himself. It is very important to the court what they medialize.

The second thing is, about the Just Dessert incident, there was a white boy who shot another person, and he was shown with a gun before he shot someone, with the gun? After that, that picture disappeared, and we have never heard what happened to that young man and how the case went. The last thing we heard was that he was living in Metro Housing, meaning he is poor, he is an aberration in the white realm.

The last point I want to make is that we can take some of the institutions to courts, despite some of the problems we encounter there. Right now I have taken the *Toronto Sun* to court for libel. They libelled my client. They put a picture with the title: "Career Criminal". And that was part of the Jamaican organized crime. They had absolutely no evidence. And then they conspired with the police, the immigration, *Toronto Sun* reporter and some other people ... All the information the compiled is confidential. It should never have been released from the police, and the immigration should never have released that information to the *Sun*. So I am suing them for libel. And they have come up with the big guns. So if you have a case in court where you are going to be up against the powers of these institutions, I think you should let us know so that we can assist in fighting the cause.

MIGUNA MIGUNA: The last contribution from the back.
UNIDENTIFIED SPEAKER: Where do we go from here?

MIGUNA MIGUNA: I don't know how to answer that, but what I can say is this, we have specific recommendations. My suggestion is that people put down their names and what they want to work on, because I know that I am a writer, I am a lawyer. Those are the things that perhaps I would immediately work on. Other people might be singers or musicians; they might want to work around music. Now, it's that concept of collective leadership that should guide us. If Otis is interested in music and we have musicians here and they can co-ordinate something and we link up, even though I work in the literary field, then we link up and we move ahead.

Now, it's on that basis that I think we should deal with this. And I think I would also encourage people to take part in BADC. One is that I personally have been secretly critical of BADC. I have never told anybody; I have never even told Mr. Laws. But you see, the best thing to do -- I don't normally criticize groups outside the group. I would join and criticize it then. It is unfair, because the group can't respond. You just go around spreading rumours, and what does the group do. So the best thing is, I will go to the meeting and I will tell them my concerns. That strengthen's the group. Let us be accountable, let us be open. That's the only way we can work.

Dudley Laws says that a national organization can't work. Perhaps we should try again. The thing is that, Black Action Defense Committee works very effectively in Toronto, but when it was Francois in Montreal was killed, there was a group there, and they did some good work, and I know that Dudley Laws had communications with them and all that. That's solidarity building. We don't have to be living in the same place to do that. And the shooting of Blacks is happening all over the place. And that's what we need to do. We have expertise and skills, we have lawyers here, we have journalists, we have our educators, we have community workers, we have people who work in various institutions. These are skills that we need and we ought to use, and we are going to use them now. And it is that that we must do right from now. If somebody does not see that as a great achievement, then I don't know what achievements are, because we cannot construct a palace out of nothing, you know, on dust. We have to start pouring water on that dust, making it into soil, and then from that soil we grew the seed and then the seed grows. We can't have the fruit just like that of dust. Right now what we have is dust. Yes, we have dust and we have sprinkles of water here and there, and we have growth here and there, but we don't have the trees yet. And let's plant that tree.

Finally, as a writer, I have to promote my book. I have a book out there, anybody who wants to buy them, they are for sale.

Thank you very much for being here. If anybody wants to have the last word, I am open.

UNIDENTIFIED SPEAKER: There is something somebody said about U of T, that he had a problem there. Well, I have been in this country a long time, and I left here and I went to the states, and I was living in the States. And my sister used to come here a long time ago, and a lot of them used to have problems, and they complained that there was racism, and nobody believed them. I know they have problems with the Human Rights, but it has had it's problems, and some things have not been taken care of. But there are a lot of nurses who used to walk away when they had problems with, you know, the cleaks, and the rules for one set and rules for another set. They all eventually filed complaints. And when they started complaining they realized that something was wrong. And they made headways the other day, and a group of them from North York, they won the case. And there is still more going on. And the authorities are very concerned about what has been going on in these hospitals. So we mustn't give up.

MUNYONZWE HAMALENGWA: I would just like to announce that we hope to transcribe these proceedings. I am taking away the cassette tapes. So down the road you will be informed about the outcome of this proceeding, and you will be informed of the progress we are making implementing some of the issues that we have announced today.

MIGUNA MIGUNA: And we will leave our numbers and you could call, because I think that's also a good thing.

UNIDENTIFIED SPEAKER: I would like to make a question and not a question. I am going to say that this meeting has been quite enlightening for me, and I am sure for all of us, I hope. And I would like to say that we need this to be -- instead of just once in a while, periodically. We need it to be on an ongoing basis, and we definitely need to get more people from the community out. Therefore, I would like to ask when is the next meeting, when are we planning to have it?
MUNYONZWE HAMALENGWA: Let the group decide. We have waited long enough.

(Some cross-discussions)

Maybe in a month. Let's commit to a month.

UNIDENTIFIED SPEAKER: Well, actually, I don't know if this has been said before, but I just want to acknowledge Miguna and Munyonzwe for the work they have done getting this meeting together.

I don't know who else have worked on this actually. I want to acknowledge Dudley and Otis and the other speakers today. But particularly Miguna and Munyonzwe are two men in our community that have worked hard. Their commitment is absolutely overwhelming. I absolutely love you guys, and we just want you to know that we are counting on you to carry on and to lead us uncompromisingly.

DUDLEY LAWS: I would just like to say that the Black Action Defense is open for membership. I do not believe that we are just keeping this organization for ourselves, right. Our phone number is 656-2232, okay. Give us a call. We meet every Wednesday at 393 Vaughan. And, you know, we have emergency meetings to discuss, you know, urgent matters of the community. Thank you very much.

--- WHEREUPON THE MEETING ENDED.

CHAPTER 4

PRELUDE TO CLASS ACTION LAW SUITS (2012)

Tribute to Charles Roach and Dudley Laws - September 9th, 2012

Dr. Munyonzwe Hamalengwa

Charles Roach has usually been ahead of his time and the times of others. Long before the enactment of the *Class Proceedings Act* in Ontario and the now commonly invoked application of universal jurisdiction (some form of global class action suits), Charles Roach had the idea that to contend against the powers-that-be, marginalized groups ought to engage in Class Action lawsuits in order to have a fair fighting chance. His vision for this was not limited to legal actions alone, he extended this idea to the very praxis of political action. One person political acts rarely produce results unless you are a Mahatma Gandhi or a

Nelson Mandela. Even these icons were backed and were part of massive political movements – the Indian Congress Party and the African National Congress. If one man political acts rarely produce results, how could one person legal actions that seek to address and redress systemic and historically evolving and embedded oppressive and discriminatory systems produce positive results?

To that end, Charles Roach has always been part of broader political and legal coalitions. Where there were no coalitions, Charles tried to found one or be part of a founding group. He did this to mention a few, founded or was part of the founding group of: BLACK ACTION DEFENSE COMMITTEE; AFRICAN CANADIAN LEGAL CLINIC; LAWYERS AGAISNT APARTHEID; NATIONAL CONFERENCE OF BLACK LAWYERS; DELOS DAVIES LAW GUILD; NAKUMBUKA and numerous others.

Charles envisioned developing legal entities that would embark on class action lawsuits along the lines trail-blazed by the Legal Fund of the National Association for the Advancement of Coloured People (NAACP); the American Civil Liberties Union (ACLU) and others including the Canadian Women's Legal Education and Action

Fund (LEAF). It has to be noted that all the other groups got the idea of forming Class oriented legal action funds/groups from the NAACP. Backed by this fund and leading this fund, Thurgood Marshall, the first black appointed to the US Supreme Court in 1967, won 29 out of 32 cases he argued there. That percentage of that winning record remains to be bested up to now. Not even governments secure as many victories as Marshall did. It is inconceivable that Marshall would have won those victories without being part of a larger well-resourced and researched group, fighting for just causes.

It goes the same for the victories secured by LEAF, the ACLU and the Centre for Constitutional Rights (CCR) and numerous other groups around the world. Judges are inclined to give victories to well financially endowed and well researched organizations and institutions, especially when dealing with systemic and wide spread discriminations or class/group etc., grievances.

In Canada, African Canadians have historic and systemic grievances including Racial Profiling, propensity to be declared as "Posing Danger to the Public in Canada", declarations of being "Serious Criminals" "Delinquents" of being marginalized in employment and in education and health care matters; Blacks are usually criminally tried by all-white juries with attendant potential biases, Blacks are underrepresented in the judiciary; there is systemic racial discrimination against Blacks which even judges have acknowledged, as have almost all independent studies. Black children are more likely to be taken away by Children's Aid Societies than other children and many other grievances.

Despite these systemic problems afflicting Blacks in Canada, Blacks have not won a single victory in the Supreme Court of Canada when some of these issues have been litigated there, I e. Racial Profiling; danger to the public etc. Challenge for cause has been allowed but not proportional representation of Blacks on jury panels. The latter is more important than the ability to challenge for cause because if the entire jury pool is white and you challenge all white jurors but still end up with 12 white jurors, what have you really accomplished? The Supreme Court of Canada has ruled in *Golden* that Blacks and Aboriginals are more likely to be strip-searched than others, yet racial profiling that leads to strip searches, has not been outlawed. Then what kind of victory is this? Look at the victories other Charter-identified groups have secured: Pay

Equity for women has been secured; discrimination in employment for women and disabled has been eliminated; natives can receive less sentences for criminal conduct; gays and lesbians can marry; maternity leave is a reality; there are now over 40% white female judges in most levels of courts etc. Yet Racial Profiling and other afflictions pertaining to Blacks have not been outlawed. One solution is to have judicial diversity by putting judges who would understand the embedded injustices facing African-Canadians.

Most of the victories secured by these other groups were secured because they were class actions lawsuits or were suits in which a great number of similarly oriented groups intervened in support of these causes and the media was similarly positively engaged. The legislative support system was also involved. On the other hand, almost all issues ventilated to promote the justice perspectives of Black Canadians were or are struggles waged by single litigants or with limited, if any interventions by any groups including our won ACLC.

Research has conclusively shown that in this day and age, only class actions law suits succeed when confronting systemic issues. Public interest groups also do not pay costs that are another advantage in addition to the advantage of equality of arms and the enhanced fire-power in class action law suits.

In the 1990s Charles wanted to bring a class action lawsuit against apartheid criminals in Canada. Charles was one of the founders of Lawyers against Apartheid. Fortunately for Apartheid Criminals in Canada, Apartheid was dismantled before we could put the research I had done to use. Charles and others founded the BADC with a view to having a resolute group that would compel the system to reform the way police treated Blacks, one of the results being the formation of the Special Investigations Unit, of whose limitations I have written about elsewhere; Charles and others founded the ACLC in order to have a group that would bring class action lawsuits against systemic discrimination; Charles founded Nakumbuka (Remembrance) in order to be part of the world-wide movement to engineer a class action lawsuit for reparations for slavery.
Charles was thinking ahead of his time. Charles began to engage in class action lawsuits against discrimination of our people in Metro housing and in schools. He began to build his firm as a social justice centre for class actions against systemic discrimination.

When I ran for Mayor of Toronto in 1997, I brought a class action lawsuit with Charles as my lawyer to strike down the prohibition of landed immigrants from voting in municipal elections. The Charter only prohibits permanent residents from voting in provincial and federal elections but not in municipal elections. What is not constitutionally prohibited is constitutionally permitted. Other lesser prohibitions like municipal ones should yield to the constitution. Permanent residents pay taxes and otherwise enjoy all privileges and burdens of being in Canada, some have been here for over fifty years, yet cannot vote in municipal elections despite the lack of constitutional prohibition. That is still an outstanding issue.

At my talk on Saturday September 8th, 2012 at the 24th Anniversary of the Founding of the BADC and at which Charles Roach was honoured for his gallantry and service to the community, I proposed that a fund be created to engage in class action lawsuits to fight systemic injustices. I am now putting that call and suggestion, in formal writing and I urge all of us to meet soon to consider this proposal with a view to putting it into action.

I have recently published an 589-page book, entitled, *The Politics of Judicial Diversity and Transformation: Canada, US, UK, Australia, Israel, South Africa, Colonial and Post-colonial Countries and International Tribunals* (2012) where some of the ideas in this proposal are distilled.

Action is awaited. Please distribute widely. Charles has built a legacy. Charles Roach's legacy has to be continued. There is no better way than to continue his "obsession" for the realization of a social justice class action-based public interest litigation model: the best model with the best chance to produce positive results against systemic and historically embedded injustices.

CHAPTER 5

LETTER TO MINISTER OF JUSTICE, BOB NICHOLSON (2010)

Dr. Munyonzwe Hamalengwa
(August 10, 2010)

Dear HonourableJustice Minister Nicholson:

Re: Legislative Act to Protect Victims of Crime

I listened with keen interest to your interview statements on CBC Morning on Monday, July 25th, 2010. You stated that your government has engaged in a blizzard of criminal legislation in order to protect the interests of victims of crime. Those victims of crime need to feel protected.

I wish to draw your attention to the existence of unheard-of and unprotected victims of racial profiling. In a recent submission on this topic, a copy of which I sent to you and other dignitaries, I quoted from various studies and judicial opinions on the impact of racial profiling on its victims. The impact is overwhelming. It is economic, psychological, social, mental and physical. It is as devastating on the victims as those victims whom you are trying to protect in your legislative agenda.

I am therefore asking you to introduce legislation to protect the victims of racial profiling. Other protective measures can also be protected. For example, the Commission of Inquiry into the Wrongful Conviction of Donald Marshal in Nova Scotia came up with some of the following recommendations, to reduce the phenomenon of racial profiling in the criminal justice system. These could be useful measures at the federal level. The Commission recommended among others:

Recommendation 9: We recommend that the Departments of the Attorney-General and Solicitor General adopt and publicize a Policy on Race Relations that has as its basis a commitment to employment equity and the elimination of inequalities, based on race, in these Departments and their agencies and the reduction of racial tensions between the Departments and the communities with which they interact.

Recommendation 10: We recommend that a Cabinet Committee on Race Relations be established which could include the Attorney-General and Solicitor-General. This Committee should meet regularly with representatives of visible minority groups in order to assure the input of these groups in matters of criminal justice.

Recommendation 12: We recommend that Governments consider the needs of visible minorities by appointing qualified visible minority judges and administrative board members whenever possible.

Recommendation 13: We recommend that the Dalhousie Law School, the Nova Scotia Barristers Society and the Judicial Councils support courses and programs dealing with legal issues facing visible minorities, and encourage sensitivity to minority concerns for law students, lawyers and judges.

Recommendation 14: We recommend that the Attorney-General establish continuing professional education programs for Crown prosecutors, which would include:

an exposure to materials explaining the nature of systematic discrimination towards Black and Native peoples in Nova Scotia in criminal justice system; and
an exploration of means by which Crown prosecutors can carry out their functions so as to reduce the effects of systematic discrimination in the Nova Scotia criminal justice system

Recommendation 15: We recommend that training for all police officers, both at the intake level and as continuing education, include content on police/minority concerns and sensitivity to visible minority issues.

Recommendation 33: We recommend that the Chief Justices and the Chief Judges of each court in Nova Scotia exercise leadership within his or her area of responsibility to ensure fair treatment of visible minorities in the criminal justice system.

The Federal Government is the only constitutionally competent authority to legislate in matters of criminal law and in which racial profiling is embedded. The Federal Government is also the primary body that is competent to implement the dictates of International Conventions or the treaties which Canada has ratified that prevent discrimination and racial profiling.

Section 15 and 27 of the *Charter* also direct the Federal Government to take a lead role in designing legislation that promote equality and prevent discrimination and racial profiling.

Thank you for considering the matters raised herein.

Yours truly,
Munyonzwe Hamalengwa

CHAPTER 6

FACT SHEET ON POLICE VIOLENCE AGAINST THE AFRICAN COMMUNITY IN CANADA

Dr. Ajamu Nangwaya

On April 6, 1911, W. F. Witsue, an Afrikan man, was arrested for allegedly stealing a diamond ring and money from the home of a White family in Edmonton, Alberta. A 15-year-old White girl, Hazel Huff, claimed that she was assaulted and drugged by Mr. Witsue. She also asserted that she had no idea what happened to her while unconscious. This incident took place during a period of white supremacist hysteria by White Canadians and their governments over Afrikan American and Afrikan Caribbean immigration into Canada. It was later revealed that the young woman made up the incident:

Nine days after initial reports of Hazel's maltreatment at the hands of black intruder, the young white woman confessed that her entire story had been a racial red herring. Huff admitted that, fearing punishment for losing her mother's ring, she fabricated the attack by a big "big, burly nigger," specifically because of the outcry over black immigration.

The chief of police in the city of Edmonton was aware of this lie seven days before Hazel's public confession, but he and her family wanted to whip up anti-Afrikan immigration excitement. It was their hope that the federal government would be pressured into further restricting the presence of Afrikans in Canada.

On July 19, 1952, Clarence Clemons, a longshoreman, was beaten and arrested by White police officers in Vancouver, British Columbia. He was later admitted to hospital and went into a coma. Clarence did not make it out of the hospital alive; died on December 24, 1952. The police officers were cleared of any wrongdoing by an all-white male jury at a coroner's inquest into the cause of Clarence's death.

On August 9, 1978, 24-year-old Buddy Evans was killed by White police officer John Clark at a Toronto nightclub on King Street West. Evan's killer was exonerated by a coroner's inquest, which lasted for 11 weeks and cost the city the princely sum of $200,000. The Afrikan community mobilized against this act of police violence. A protest rally "sponsored by the Sikh-led Action Committee Against Racism" attracted between 1,200 – 2,000 demonstrators.

On August 26, 1979, 35-year-old Albert Johnson was shot to death in his apartment. Two White police officers, William Inglis and Walter Cargnelli, were charged with manslaughter in this killing. Johnson's killers were acquitted in November 1980.

On November 11, 1987, 19-year-old unarmed Anthony Griffins was shot in the head and killed by White police officer Allan Gosset in a Montreal police station parking lot. Griffin's killer was acquitted of criminal negligence in 1994. Anthony's mother Gloria Augustus was later given $27,000 in compensation for the killing of her son. Anthony's killer, Allan Gosset, had a charge of racism levied against him in 1981 and he forfeited $2,000 to the victim of his racist behaviour.

On August 9, 1988, 44-year-old Lester Donaldson was shot to death in his rooming house apartment in Toronto by White police officer David Deviney. The killer cop was acquitted of any wrongdoing for this shooting death. But in 1998, Lester Donaldson's killer was found guilty of uttering the racist slurs "apes" and "f---ing n-----s" in an internal police investigative process, which was carried out under the Police Services Act.

In August 1988, the Black Action Defense Committee (BADC) was formed in the wake of the killing of Lester Donaldson by killer cop David Diveny. Some of the organization's co-founders were Charles Roach, Sherona Hall, Dudley Laws, Akua Benjamin and Lennox Farrell. BADC went on to become the premier police accountability and community resistance organization in the Toronto region and Ontario.

On December 8, 1988, Michael Wade Lawson, a 17-year-old Mississauga (Ontario) teenager, was shot in the back of his head while joyriding in a stolen car. Two White police officers Anthony Lelaragni and Darren Longpre were charged with manslaughter and aggravated assault, respectively. Michael's killers were acquitted by an all-white jury on April 7, 1992. Several days later, over 300 people protested the "not guilty" verdict in downtown Toronto.

On December 13, 1988, the government of Ontario created the *Race Relation and Policing Task Force* in response to the killing of Lester Donaldson and Michael Wade Lawson. Clare Lewis, the Public Complaints Commissioner of Metropolitan Toronto, was appointed to head the task force, which was empowered with the directive "to address promptly the very serious concerns of visible minority communities respecting the interaction of the police community with their own." The organizing, mobilizing and public education work of the Afrikan community and allies prompted this action from the Ontario government. Two moderates from the Afrikan community were appointed to the task force: Dr. Ralph Agard and Roy Williams.

In April 1989, the *Race Relations and Policing Task Force* submitted *The Report of the Race Relations and Policing task Force* to the government of Ontario.

On April 25, 1989, Denny Dias, an African Canadian cop, submitted a secret intelligence report on his surveillance of 13 activist and civil rights organizations and 18 individuals from the African community in Toronto. The secret police spied on groups such as the National Council of Jamaicans, Coalition of Visible Minority Women, Justice for Wade Lawson Committee, and National Black Coalition of Canada and individuals such as Dudley Laws, Ras Rico I, Dari Meade, Dr. Wilson Head, Kamala-Jean Gopie, Evelyn Lennon-Lyon (Michael Wade Lawson's mother) and Greg Bobb. None of the individuals who were targeted by the secret police had a criminal conviction.

On October 27, 1989, 23-year-old Brampton resident Sophia Cook was shot in the back while strapped down in the passenger seat of a car. The bullet was fired by White police officer Cameron Durham and it temporarily paralyzed Sophia. She had taken a ride in a car after missing her bus. It was later reported that the car was stolen, but Sophia never had any prior criminal engagement with the law. Constable Durham was acquitted of the charge of careless use of a firearm in 1994.

On April 9, 1990, 26-year-old Montreal resident Leslie Presley was shot six times at the Thunderdome nightclub. The three White cops Jean Chatigny, Daniel Rousseau and Jean Pellerin who were involved in Leslie's killing were cleared of any wrongdoing after a coroner's inquest. The Sûreté du Québec had also absolved the killers.

On May 14, 1990, unarmed 16-year-old Marlon Neal was shot after fleeing a police radar trap in Scarborough. White police officer Brian Rapson was found not guilty in 1991 of the charges of criminal negligence causing bodily harm, attempted murder and aggravated assault.

In August 1990, the Special Investigations Unit (SIU) was proclaimed by the new Police Services Act in Ontario and this body was charged with the responsibility of carrying out "criminal investigations into circumstances involving police and civilians that have resulted in serious injury, death or allegations of sexual assault." This independent investigatory body is staffed by former police officers and the community does not view it as being sufficiently distanced from the police that it is called upon to scrutinize.

In May 1991, the Metro Toronto Police Association attempted to muzzle Dudley Laws by launching a multi-million dollar defamation lawsuit against him for asserting that Toronto's cops were "the most brutal and murderous in North America." The police quietly dropped the libel lawsuit in April 1994, although it was set for trial in May 1994.

In May 1991, the Metro Toronto Police Association launched a public campaign aimed at silencing Police Services Board member Roy Williams, a political moderate, for his defense of Dudley Laws' freedom to share his opinion on the police and policing as well as his encouragement of the community to provide funds for Laws' legal defence against the libel lawsuit of the police union.

In October 1991, Dudley Laws was the victim of a Toronto police, Royal Canadian Mounted Police (RCMP) and United States' border police concocted immigration entrapment scheme that resulted in three charges against him for smuggling immigrants south of the border. The charges against Dudley were withdrawn in October 1998 in exchange for doing 200 hours of community service and "no record of criminal charges" after a year. It has been claimed that the police spent between $400,000 to $1,000,000 on its entrapment investigation of Dudley.

On July 3, 1991, 24 year-old Marcellus Francois was shot in the head by a SWAT-team issued rifle in Old Montreal. The police claimed that it was a case of mistaken identity and they thought Francois was a suspect after whom they were searching. The SWAT team sergeant Michel Tremblay who fired the fatal bullet was cleared of any wrongdoing by Sûreté du Québec, the provincial police, and two other officers were slapped on the wrist with suspensions of short duration for misconduct. Francois's family was given a compensation of $218,269 in settlement of a lawsuit brought against the cops for the killing of its kin.

On September 19, 1991, a 17-year-old unarmed Afrikan Canadian was shot by police officer Richard Moore, himself an Afrikan Canadian. The youth was injured after being apprehended by the cop. The unidentified teenager was a member of group of youth who were riding in a stolen van. Two months later, Moore was charged with criminal negligence causing bodily harm and careless use of a firearm, because he discharged a round from his .38-calibre revolver into the chest of the teenager. On June 23, 1993, the cop was cleared of all charges by a jury of six men and six women.

On November 9, 1991, Toronto resident 24 year-old Jonathon Howell was shot by White Detective Constable Karl Sokolowski and left permanently brain damaged. The shooter was found guilty of the charge of careless use of a firearm, in a judge-only trial and was given an absolute discharge (essentially walked out of court without a criminal record).

On December 3, 1991, Royan Bagnaut, 21, was shot in his arm and chest by White police constable Douglas Lines for allegedly stealing a purse while armed with a knife. Lines claimed that the barrage of bullets that he fired was influenced by his belief that Royan had a gun. Royan had no firearm on his person. The cop was charged with criminal negligence causing bodily harm, but was acquitted in 1993 by a jury of 11 Whites and 1 Asian.

On May 2, 1992, 22-year-old Raymond Lawrence was shot and killed by White undercover cop Robert Rice. The killer claimed that the deceased faced him with knife after a long foot chase, but Raymond's fingerprint was not found on the knife. Raymond was killed with two bullets to the chest. Raymond's killer was exonerated after a month-long investigation by the SIU.

On May 4, 1992, the *Yonge Street Uprising* emerged out of the Black Action Defence Committee-organized demonstration against the killing of Raymond Lawrence. This unprecedented rebellion against police violence led to the Ontario New Democrat government's requesting an investigation by Stephen Lewis into the root causes of the rebellion by an Afrikan-led, but multi-racial group of young people. Stephen Lewis prepared the document *Report of the Advisor on Race Relations to the Premier of Ontario, Bob Rae* and one of it main assertions was "First, what we are dealing with, at root, and fundamentally is anti-Black racism.... Just as the soothing balm of 'multiculturalism' cannot mask racism, so racism cannot mask its primary target [Afrikan people]." The *Yonge Street Uprising* led to a number of anti-racism and equity initiatives and policy changes by the government of the day.

On January 1, 1993, Montreal resident Trevor Kelly was fatally shot in the back by White police officer Richard Massé. The Surete du Quebec did the investigation and claimed that Trevor's killer was justified in shooting the Rastafari practitioner. According to Massé his partner's life was endangered by Trevor standing over him with a paring knife. No civilian witnesses were found to provide an independent account of the killing of Trevor by the cop attached to the Montreal Urban Community police. Interestingly, police investigators of the shooting death "found a kitchen knife five feet away from Kelly's body - with no fingerprints on it."

On April 20, 1993, 21-year-old Ian Clifford Coley was shot to death by a White cop, Rick Shank, of 41 Division. Clifford was shot twice in the chest and his killer was cleared of any wrongdoing by the SIU. **On March 30, 1997**, Shank killed unarmed Hugh Dawson. Nine bullets were pumped into Hugh's body within four seconds.

On August 10, 1993, 37-year-old Audrey Smith, a tourist, public sector worker and mother of five from Jamaica, was strip-searched "naked as the day I was born, on the street" in downtown Toronto. Audrey was accused of having drugs in her possession. She was immediately handcuffed and placed in a cruiser. After being detained and the cops ignoring her assertion that she was innocent, Audrey thought that her only option was to consent to a search, presumably at a police station. Instead Audrey was strip-searched on a busy Parkdale neighbourhood street. No drugs were found on her. The names of the White cops who were involved in this act of humiliation and public violence are Constables Tracey Peters, Michael Sommer and Michael Dulmage.

As if Audrey's humiliation at the hands of Canadian authority wasn't enough, Canadian "immigration officials ordered Air Canada to drag her out of the airport departure lounge in her native Kingston, Jamaica" in April 1994. The irony of this incidence was the fact that she was on her way to attend the inquiry into her 1993 strip-search complaint. Faulty intelligence was given as the reason behind her mistreatment at the airport. A three-person panel of inquiry cleared the three cops of discreditable conduct charges in September 1995, while carrying out a hatchet-job on Audrey's character and reputation. Audrey had this to say about the decision "Just because I stood up for my rights I have been called a prostitute, a drug dealer. They (the police officers) treated me like a dog. And now the panel is backing them. I can't believe this. This is not justice."

On October 23, 1993, 27-year-old Dwight Drummond, an assignment editor with popular media outlet City TV and Ron Allen were the victims of a "high risk takedown" by Metro Toronto police. Ron and Dwight "were ordered at gunpoint from their car, forced to kneel and lie on the ground, and their car was searched." The cops claimed that they matched the description of two Afrikan men who were earlier seen with a gun. A "phantom" sex trade worker was the source of the preceding allegation. In 1995, a board of inquiry exonerated White police officers Mark Hannah and David Smith who were charged under the *Police Services Act* with behaving "in a disorderly manner, or in a manner prejudicial to discipline or likely to bring discredit upon the reputation of the police force." Dwight declared at a news conference that the dismissal of the charges was an undisguised declaration of an "open season" on Afrikan men.

On September 29, 1994, Albert Moses, 41, was killed in his room in downtown Toronto. A White cop, Jeffrey Vance, shot Albert in his face and alleged that the latter attacked his partner with a hammer. The SIU cleared the killer of any wrongdoing.

In October 1994, Arnold Minors, a progressive Afrikan man, was mercilessly demonized by Toronto's police, police boosters, people from the legal profession, elements within the mass media and politicians for saying that many Afrikan Canadians do not collaborate with the police in their investigations, because they are seen as "occupation armies" in the community. He was a member of the Toronto Police Services Board at the time when he was being relentlessly ostracized by the police and the media.

On January 10, 1996, Tommy Anthony Barnett, 22, shot to death by White police sergeant Benedetto Troina in the Bathurst and St. Clair area of Toronto. The police claimed that Tommy was unsheathing a sword. Troina fired four bullets into Tommy's chest. Tommy's killer was cleared of any wrongdoing by the SIU.

On March 14, 1996, Andrew Bramwell, 24, was shot to death by White constable Andy Kis in the Jane and Finch area. The officer fired three bullets into Andrew's lower back and one in the back of one of his thighs and an unfired Glock pistol was recovered from the scene. Kis was cleared of criminal wrongdoing in the fatal shooting of Andrew by the SIU.

On June 11, 1996, 24-year-old Seneca College student Wayne Rick Williams was shot to death by Kenneth Harrison (his second fatal shooting) and Gordon Hayford. Wayne experienced depression and schizophrenia. It was claimed that Wayne had a knife in his hand in the driveway of his home when multiple shoots were fired at him. An autopsy revealed that four bullets entered Wayne's body. The SIU cleared the officers of any wrongdoing in the fatal shooting. But a coroner's jury returned a verdict of homicide (does not assign blame) in June 2000 and dismissed the suggestion that Wayne was intentionally courting death when he was shot.

On March 30, 1997, White police officer Rick Shank killed unarmed 31-year-old Hugh Dawson while he was sitting at the steering wheel of his car and strapped down with the seatbelt. Shank fired a total of nine bullets into Hugh's body. It was reported that firearm's examiner Michael Clarke revealed at the trial that the "muzzle of the pistol was about one to three inches from Dawson when it was fired, leaving powder burns on his clothing". The police claimed that High grabbed Shank's and another officer's guns, but Hugh's fingerprints weren't found on the guns in question. On May 25, 1999, a jury of six men and six women cleared Shank of a manslaughter charge in the killing of Hugh.

On December 31, 1999, Henry Musaka, 26, was fatally shot twice in the head and once in the chest by Toronto's emergency task force officers responding to an allegation that the victim had taken a hostage, a St. Michael Hospital emergency room doctor. The officers James Bremner and Chris Lussow were involved in the shooting. The police recovered an unloaded pellet gun from the deceased. Henry went to seek treatment for his son who was having trouble with his breathing. But Henry was told that a pediatrician was not available and a doctor would see his son in an hour's time. This seemingly uncaring attitude toward Henry's son's welfare prompted the hostage-taking action.

On October 8, 2002, 19-year-old Brendan Clarke was brutalized by two police officers from the Royal Canadian Mounted Police (RCMP) Geoff Quibell and Jamall Gray in a convenient store where he went to purchase a packet of chewing gum. He gave the store clerk a $100 bill. The person thought it was a counterfeit bill and called the police. The money was a legitimate legal tender.

Brendan was battered by Quibell, the main aggressor and was charged for resisting arrest, causing a disturbance and assaulting a police officer. Most of the battering took place on the store's surveillance camera. The cops deliberately moved Brendan away from the coverage area of the camera while punching and manhandling him. The victim of police violence was convicted on the charge of disturbing the peace.

Brendan launched a lawsuit against the Attorney General of Canada, the RCMP's commissioner and constable Geoff Quibell. On June 17, 2013, the Supreme Court of Nova Scotia court signed-off on the federal government's and Brendan's out-of-court settlement, which gave him a monetary compensation of $248,000 and "letter of regret" from the RCMP for the assault on him.

On October 19, 2002, the *Toronto Star* published the findings of its landmark investigation into police racial profiling in Toronto. It obtained access to a police database that recorded 480,000 incidents of police contact with civilians from 1996 to 2001, which generated a ticket or arrest. It was clearly established that Afrikans received racially differential treatment from the police.

The Star's report uncovered the following racist police practices:

Most people charged with simple drug possession were free to go home, on a promise to appear in court and at a police station. Whites were released on the scene 76.5 per cent of the time while blacks were released 61.8 per cent of the time.

The difference in treatment was even more apparent at the next level of police decision-

making. Of those taken to the station, blacks were held behind bars for a court appearance 15.5 per cent of the time. Whites were kept in jail awaiting a bail hearing in 7.3 per cent of cases.

The Toronto Star's investigation also uncovered the existence of the "DWB or Driving While Black" phenomenon wherein Afrikans were disproportionately charged for "out-of-sight" offences such as failing to update a driver's licence or driving without insurance." The newspaper asserts, "Police usually discover such violations only after a motorist has been pulled over. And, in the absence of any other charge, it isn't clear why drivers involved in these offences are stopped in the first place."

On August 4, 2003, 21-year old Said JamaJama, a Somali immigrant, was arrested for assaulting a cop and causing a disturbance in the North-West area of Rexdale, Toronto. The fabricated charges against Jama was exposed by a tourist from Ottawa who videotaped the incident. Jama was brutalized by White 6-year veteran Roy Preston. The former appeared in the video with his hands down and in a non-threatening posture when the cop gave him a roundhouse punch to the jaw. The surfacing of the video led to the dismissal of the bogus charges against Jama by the crown attorney.

The cop was convicted for assault on July 28, 2005 and he appealed the conviction. The lower court's decision was upheld on November 16, 2007 and the cop was led off to jail to serve his 30-day sentence. The cop had the privilege of serving the sentence on weekends. In the absence of the video-recording of the violent behaviour of the cop, it is likely that Jama would have been convicted, imprisoned and later deported from Canada.

On March 9, 2005, Canada Post letter carrier Ron Phipps was racially profiled by White Constable Shaw of 33 Division police station, while working in the affluent Bridle Path neighbourhood. The racist cop stopped, questioned and followed Ron and sought verification of his identity from a White letter carrier.

Ron took his case to the *Human Rights Tribunal of Ontario* and adjudicator Kaye Joachim found the cop guilty of racial profiling. In rendering her judgment, Joachim states, "I do not accept Const. Shaw's evidence that the applicant was crossing the street back and forth in an unusual fashion. Const. Shaw was well aware that letter carriers do not stop at every house. It was not unusual to miss deliver mail and to go back and try to retrieve it.

"The fact that it was an African-Canadian male without a vehicle that attracted Const. Shaw's attention is what is unusual...." **On March 13, 2012**, the *Ontario Court Appeal* upheld the racial profiling judgment of the tribunal.

On May 29, 2005, 18-year-old Chad Aiken, an Afrikan Canadian, was driving his mother's white Mercedes in Ottawa with his mostly Afrikan Canadian friends. An oncoming patrol turned around on seeing Chad and his friends in the car and later signaled for him to stop. Chad asked the officer for his name and badge number and the officer lied that it was "666" and his name was "Holland." The cop taunted Chad and hit him in his chest. An audio-recording of the confrontation was done by Chad's girlfriend by way of a cell phone. The police officer gave Chad "a ticket for a burnt out light over his car's licence plate."

Chad took the Ottawa Police Service to the Ontario Human Rights Commission for the cops' racial profiling action. In 2010, a confidential settlement was reached between Chad and the police, which included a "letter of regret" and quite likely a financial settlement. A 2012, settlement between the police force and the human rights commission mandated the police to collect racial data during traffic stops over a two-year period. Chad and the African Canadian Legal Clinic (ACLC) disagreed with the limited scope of the data collection. ACLA lawyer Virginia Nelder asserts "If you limit the project to traffic stops, you're missing out on all of the young African Canadian men that are stopped on a daily basis just walking along the street."

On November 25, 2005, Rawle Maynar was driving in his black BMW while being followed by Toronto police constable Ryan Baker. Rawle drove onto his driveway and alighted from his vehicle and approached the cop to determine the reason why he was trailed to his house.

The cop pulled his gun and the other officers who arrived on the scene did the same. Rawle was handcuffed, placed in a police cruiser, but later released. The cops were looking for an Afrikan suspect in a in a black sports car.

Rawle took his case before the *Ontario Human Rights Tribunal* and won his racial profiling case on January 22, 2012. He was awarded $40,000, which was jointly assessed against constable Ryan Baker and the Toronto Police Services Board. In the words of adjudicator Leslie Reaume, "I do not believe that if the suspect had been a Caucasian man in the same circumstance, with no other defining characteristics, particularly age ...[that the officer] ... would have chosen to investigate the first Caucasian man he saw driving the same car at the same intersection."

On June 20, 2006, 15-year-old unarmed Duane Christian was shot to death by White constable Steve Darnley who fired five bullets, which made contact with the teenager's chest and arm. Duane was driving a stolen van. The killer claimed that Constable Rowena Edey, his partner, was in danger of being harmed by the reversing vehicle. The SIU later cleared the killer cop of wrongdoing in this fatal shooting in the Scarborough area of Toronto.

On October 6, 2007, 37-year-old Afrikan Canadian Roger Shallow, a crown attorney in Ontario, was arrested for causing a disturbance and assault to resist arrest at Toronto's 52 division police station, where he was subjected to a strip search. The arresting officers were Gail Shields, a White woman, and Paul Clarke, an Afrikan man. The charges against Roger were withdrawn because the prosecutor concluded that "there was no reasonable prospect of conviction", according to the Toronto Star.

Roger filed a racism-related complaint against the Toronto Police Services Board and five cops with the *Human Rights Tribunal of Ontario.*

On June 22, 2008, Nathaniel Fells, 19, and William Drummond, 20, were the targets of racist slurs by off-duty police officers outside a bar in Digby, Nova Scotia. This act of aggression led to a confrontation and a police from Halifax was knocked unconscious. An off-duty RCMP cop used a stun gun on Drummond and he was arrested. However, the off-duty peace officers who were involved in the racist altercation "were ushered out of the downtown area."

There's a history of racist police behaviour against members of the Afrikan community Digby. Sgt. Wylie Grim, then commanding officer of the RCMP's Digby detachment, directed sexist and racist comments at Afrikan female staff members and a colleague. On January 29, 2005, Assistant Commissioner of the RCMP Ian Atkin apologized for Grimm's transgressions, "Those things had to be acknowledged, and to demonstrate to the community that we were prepared to move forward and to work with the community in developing appropriate sensitivity strategies that would regain the trust of the community."

On September 26, 2008, 27-year-old Stacy Bonds was arrested and traumatized by Sgt. Steven Desjourdy, Melanie Morris, Cameron Downie, Michael Bednarek and John Flores from the Ottawa police force. Her rights under the Charter of Rights and Freedoms were violated. According to Justin Sadler of Sun Media, "An internal police investigation is ongoing after a judge threw out public intoxication and assault charges against Bonds, ruling Ottawa cops violently attacked her, illegally strip searched her, cut her shirt and bra off, and left her in a cold cell for three hours, half naked, after she soiled herself."

In dismissing the fictitious charge of assaulting police, the trial judge, Justice Richard Lajoie of the Ontario court of justice, had the following to say about the case,

"There is no reasonable explanation ... to have cut Ms. Bonds' shirt and bra off, and there is no reason, apart from vengeance and malice, to have left Ms. Bonds in the cell for a period of three hours and 15 minutes half naked and having soiled her pants, before she received what is called a blue suit."

On March 15, 2011, Sgt. Steven Desjourdy was charged with sexual assault stemming from his arrest of Stacy Bonds and cutting off her bra and shirt.

On December 17, 2011, Stacy Bonds launched a $1.2 million lawsuit against "the Ottawa Police Service, Chief Vern White, and Constables Melanie Morris, Steven Desjourdy, Cameron Downie, Michael Bednarek and John Flores.

On April 3, 2013, Steve Desjourdy was acquitted of the charge by Ontario Court Justice Tim Lipson.

In January 2009, Dr. Clem Marshall, a longtime Toronto-based educator and community organizer, was stopped and questioned in a Parkdale neighborhood by cops from the Toronto Police Service. Dr. Marshall was driving a 2009 Nissan Altima.

According to Dr. Marshall, one of the cops declared, "It's not racial profiling. . . . Two black guys driving a car like mine in Parkdale meant crack. . . . That's just the way it is." Clem alleged that the cops' racial animus was further confirmed after he asked them about the reason for stopping him. One of the cops declared, "Who do you think you are, f---ing Obama?"

On May 13, 2013, the Toronto Police Service and the Toronto Police Services Board settled for an undisclosed sum with Dr. Marshall. A gag order was imposed on revealing the terms of the settlement. The case was working its way through Ontario's Human Rights Tribunal when the agreement was reached.

On February 1, 2010, a story in the *Toronto Star* revealed the startling but everyday reality of Afrikans and other racialized peoples being stopped and questioned by the police, "*In each of the city's 74 police patrol zones, the* Star *analysis shows that blacks were documented at significantly higher rates than their overall census population by zone, and that in many zones, the same holds true for "brown" people — mainly people of South Asian, Arab and West Asian backgrounds.*" This information and others on race, racism and policing were compiled from data that covered the period 2003 to 2008.

The Star's investigation also revealed that police racial profiling of Afrikans in Toronto is "highest in more affluent, mostly white areas of the city, such as North Toronto and the Kingsway."

While Africans are 8.4 per cent of Toronto's population, they made up over 24 per cent of the civilians who were stopped and had their information documented on the "208 card" used by the police. Further, African boys and men between the ages of 15-24 were 2.5 times more likely to be stopped and questioned by the police than their white counterparts.

On May 5, 2010, 18-year-old Junior Alexander Manon died after a short chase by the police and while in their custody. It was initially claimed in news reports that the teenager died from a heart attack. However, lawyer Selwyn Pieter had this to say on the subject, "There was blood all over. He had a neck brace on. His eyes were black and blue. The issue of a heart attack is a fiction. It seems that he died from physical force. He was a healthy young person."

The SIU cleared the cops, Sgt. Stuart Blower and Constable Michael Adams, of any wrongdoing in the death of Junior. At the coroner's inquest, the provincial pathologist testified that the "cause of death was positional asphyxia after the chase and exertion." The inquest jury's official cause of death was attributed to "restrain asphyxia", which suggests that the cops' action stopped Junior from breathing properly, but it claimed the killing was an accident.

On August 29, 2010, a Toronto cop killed 25-year-old Reyal Jensen Jardine-Douglas, an Afrikan man with mental illness. He died from multiple gunshot wounds to his body. The police dispatcher was aware of his mental health status, because it was Reyal's family who called the police seeking help in getting him admitted to a hospital. The police claimed to have recovered a knife from the scene of the killing. The killer cop or subject officer was never publicly identified and the SIU cleared the shooter of any wrongdoing on January 27, 2011.

On September 1, 2010, 22-year-old Ohene Darteh had his rights under the Charter of Rights and Freedom violated by Constable Irwin "The Terminator" Correa of the Toronto Anti-Violence Intervention Strategy (TAVIS). "The Terminator" charged Ohene with possession of cocaine and the latter asserted that the narcotic substance was planted by the cop. Ohene was also injured by the cops.

Justice Brian O'Mara of the Ontario Supreme Court dismissed the drugs charge and found The Terminator's behaviour "intimidating, overbearing and oppressive" during the arrest and questioning of Ohene. According Toronto Star reporter Alex Ballingall, Justice "O'Marra dismissed Correa's testimony as "untruthful and unreliable," finding it "highly improbable" that Darteh would "initiate physical contact with a larger uniformed officer while two other uniformed officers are present."

On September 29, 2010, 26-year-old unarmed Eric Osawe was killed by Toronto Police Service's killer cop David Cavanagh. Eric was a father of two and was killed in an apartment in Etobicoke. After a two-month investigation by the SIU Constable Cavanagh was charged with manslaughter. It was just the third time that a cop has had such a charge levied against him by the SIU for killing a civilian. But one might not want to get his or her hopes up about justice being served. The killer cops were acquitted in the two other cases.

In February 2012, the charge against the killer cop David Cavanagh was upgraded to second degree murder and the preliminary inquiry commenced on October 1, 2012. On March 1, 2013, Provincial Court Justice Michael Block dismissed the charge against David Cavanagh at the preliminary trial and stated that the gun went off accidentally.

On February 3, 2012, Michael Eligon, a 29-year-old mentally ill Afrikan man was shot to death by a member of the Toronto police force. He was set to be released on February 3rd from a 72-hour psychiatric evaluation at the Toronto East General Hospital. Michael was shot to death with a pair of scissors in each hand. The SIU exonerated the cop of any wrongdoing in the killing of Michael.

Ontario Ombudsman Andre Marin raised serious questions about the partiality of the SIU's investigators who covered the crime scene for the supposedly independent agency. The investigators were caught on film wearing police insignia and rings as well as appearing to be in agreement with the police version of the shooting. On the latter concern, the ombudsman thought the SIU investigators arrived at the scene "a whole bunch of pre-conceived notions of self-defence."

Marin commented further on the appearance of pro-police bias, "When you have people whose family member has been shot by police and the investigators show up on scene with police badges and rings, it creates suspicion that you are not going to be treated impartially and fairly." One investigator was disciplined by way of a suspension from work and two personnel were required to undergo counselling over the display of a pro-police bias.

On February 20, 2012, Frank Anthony Berry, a 48-year-old Afrikan man, was shot to death in the west end of Toronto (on Campbell Avenue, near Dupont Street and Lansdowne Avenue). The SIU investigated this cop killing in which one subject officer (the killer cop) and seven subject officers (cops on the scene of the killing) were implicated.

The police discharged two bullets in Frank's torso because they claim that he approached them with a knife, which was later found to be a pair of scissors. The SIU cleared the killer cop of any wrongdoing.

On March 10, 2012, the Toronto Star published the first story in the series *Known to Police*. The series exposed the extent to which Afrikan must contend with the structural violence of police containment, surveillance and repression:

"While blacks make up 8.3 per cent of Toronto's population, they accounted for 25 per cent of the cards filled out between 2008 and mid-2011. In each of the city's 72 patrol zones, blacks are more likely than whites to be stopped and carded. The

likelihood increases in areas that are predominantly white."

In November 2014, the consulting firm Logical Outcomes published the research report *"This issue has been with us for ages": A community-based Assessment of Police Contact carding in 31 Division* on the carding practices of Toronto's cops in the racialized, working-class community of Jane and Finch community. In spite of the supposedly human rights-informed April 2014 Community Contact Policy on carding, significant majorities of respondents had experiences, which were in violation of the current policy (see page 42). Seventy-one percent (71%) of the carded individuals were Afrikan Canadians.

CHAPTER 7

A FACTUM ON THE APPLICATION FOR CERTIFICATION OF A RACIAL PROFILING CLASS ACTION LAW SUIT

Dr. Munyonzwe Hamalengwa

INTRODUCTION

In this matter, the representative plaintiffs wish to bring a class action proceeding against the Toronto Police and related defendants for the racial profiling of African Canadian residents of the Toronto region. It appears to be inarguable that African Canadians are stopped, asked for identification, and searched at a much higher rate than other persons.

The issue is essentially whether a claim may be brought for damages, injunctive relief, and a declaratory order by means of class action proceedings in the circumstances set out above.

STATUTORY FRAMEWORK

The Class Proceedings Act, 1992, S.O. 1992, c. 6, s. 5(1), (2) provides that the court shall certify a class proceeding if (a) the pleadings or the notice of application discloses a cause of action; (b) there is an identifiable class of two or more persons that would be represented by the representative plaintiff or defendant; (c) the claims or defences of the class members raise common issues; (d) a class proceeding would be the preferable procedure for the resolution of the common issues; and (e) there is a representative plaintiff or defendant who: (i) would fairly and adequately represent the interests of the class; (ii) has produced a plan for the proceeding that sets out a workable method of advancing the proceeding on behalf of the class and of notifying class members of the proceeding; and (iii) does not have, on the common issues for the class, an interest in conflict with the interests of other class members. Notwithstanding the aforementioned provision, where a class includes a subclass whose members have claims or defences that raise common issues not shared by all the class members, so that, in the opinion of the court, the protection of the interests of the subclass members requires that they be separately represented, the court shall not certify the class proceedings unless there is a representative plaintiff or defendant who (a) would fairly and adequately represent the interests of the subclass; (b) has produced a plan for the proceeding that sets out a workable method of advancing the proceeding on behalf of the subclass and of notifying subclass members of the proceeding; and (c) does not have, on the common issues for the subclass, an interest in conflict with the interests of other subclass members.

And furthermore, the court shall not refuse to certify a proceeding as a class proceeding solely on any of the following grounds: (1) the relief claimed includes a claim for damages that would require individual assessment after determination of the common issues; (2) the relief claimed related to separate contracts involving different class members; (3) different remedies are sought for different class members; (4) the number of class members or the identity of each class member is not known; (5) the class includes a subclass whose members have claims or defences that raise common issues not shared by all class members.

DISCLOSURE OF A CAUSE OF ACTION

As noted above, before a court can certify a class proceeding, the first requirement is that the pleadings or the notice of application must disclose a cause of action.

The certification stage, however, is not meant to be a test of the merits of the action. The question is not whether the claim is likely to succeed but whether the action is appropriate as a class proceeding.

Reference: Hollick v. Metropolitan Toronto (Municipality) (2001), 13 C.P.C. (5th) 1 (S.C.C.) (proposed class action concerning environmental pollution to neighbouring properties caused by large garbage dump; not disputed that cause of action existing).

The test is whether it is plain and obvious that the claim cannot succeed.

Reference: Buffett v. Ontario (Attorney General) (1998), 27 C.P.C. (4th) 282 (Ont. Gen. Div.) (proposed class action for declaration that provincial law contrary to Charter of Rights disclosed a cause of action but not certified as not preferable procedure); 909787 Ontario Ltd. v.

Bulk Barn Foods Ltd. (2000), 2 C.P.C. (5th) 61 (Ont. Div. Ct.) (proposed class action by franchisee for breach of contract by franchisor; only evidence of possible breach consisted of two old incidents not amounting to breach).

This test is analogous to that which applies when determining whether a statement of claim should be struck as disclosing no cause of action.

Reference: Ontario Rules of Civil Procedure, R.R.O. 1990, Reg. 194, R. 21 [am. O. Reg. 171/98, s. 6; O. Reg. 206/02, s. 5; O. Reg. 14/04, s. 15]; Peppiatt v. Nicol (1993), 20 C.P.C. (3d) 272 (Ont. Gen. Div.) (pleadings disclosed a cause of action based on negligent misrepresentation and breach of fiduciary duty);Anderson v. Wilson (1999), 36 C.P.C. (4th) 17 (Ont. C.A.); leave to appeal refused (2000), 258 N.R. 194 (note) (S.C.C.) (cause of action certified for medical negligence and nervous shock as not plain and obvious at certification stage that tort of mental distress would fail); Delgrosso v. Paul (1999), 41 C.P.C. (4th) 390(Ont. Gen. Div.); leave to appeal refused (1999), 46 C.P.C. (4th) 140 (Ont. Div. Ct.) (claim certified as class action against solicitor based not on duty between solicitor and client but solicitor having placed himself in such proximity to third party that not plain and obvious that no duty of care owed); Ormrod v. Etobicoke (City) Hydro-Electric Commission (2001), 3 C.P.C. (5th) 253 (Ont. S.C.J.) (cause of action existing as not plain and obvious from pleadings that plaintiff would not succeed in claim concerning employer's lack of right to terminate premium sharing arrangement with pensioners); Cheung v. Kings Land Developments Inc. (2001), 14 C.P.C. (5th) 374 (Ont. S.C.J.); leave to appeal refused (2002), 156 O.A.C. 73(Ont. Div. Ct.) (defendants did not oppose finding that pleadings disclosed cause of action for breach of trust, breach of contract, fraud, and negligent misrepresentation concerning failed condominium project);Franklin v. University of Toronto (2001), 13 C.P.C. (5th) 340 (Ont. S.C.J.) (claim based on unjust enrichment because of breach of statute disclosing cause of action; class action for pay equity not certified as each plaintiff would still have to prove pay discrimination in each case); Chadha v. Bayer Inc. (2001), 8 C.P.C. (5th) 138 (Ont. Div. Ct.); affirmed (2003), 2003 CarswellOnt 49 (Ont. C.A.); leave to appeal refused(2003), 2003 CarswellOnt 2810 (S.C.C.) (cause of action being damages resulting from price-fixing conspiracy to raise prices of product); Williams v. Toronto (City) (2012), 2012 CarswellOnt 16441 (Ont. C.A.) (novel or unsettled issues of law should pass plain and obvious test to be determined on full evidentiary record).

In the present matter, it appears that this leg of the inquiry, namely the disclosure of a cause of action will succeed, and therefore requires no further discussion.

IDENTIFIABLE CLASS

As noted above, before a class proceeding can be certified, the second requirement is that there must be an identifiable class of two (2) or more persons who would be represented by the representative plaintiff or defendant.
Reference: Class Proceedings Act, 1992, S.O. 1992, c. 6, s. 5(1)(b).

An identifiable class exists when the class can be determined by objective criteria without reference to the merits of the action. Each member of the class does not have to be named; however, the onus is on the putative class representative to show that the class is defined sufficiently narrowly.

Reference: Hollick v. Metropolitan Toronto (Municipality) (2001), 13 C.P.C. (5th) 1 (S.C.C.) (potential class members defined as all present or past homeowners from a certain date in a defined area adjacent to large garbage dump; class sufficiently defined).

It is notable from a review of United States case-law that an entire racial group which has been subjected to a certain practice or activity by state actors may constitute a class. Thus, in Ortega-Melendres v. Arpaio 836 F.Supp.2d 959 (2011) the court certified as a class "All Latino persons who, since January, 2007, have been or will be in the future, stopped, detained, questioned or searched by MCSO agents while driving or sitting in a vehicle on a public roadway or parking area in Maricopa County, Arizona."

Likewise, in International Molders' and Allied Workers' Local Union No. 164 v. Nelson, 102 F.R.D. 457, 38 Fed.R.Serv.2d 1125, the certified class was described as "all persons of Hispanic or other Latin American ancestry, residing or working within the jurisdiction of the San Francisco District Office of the United States Immigration and Naturalization Service (INS) and/or the Livermore Border Patrol Sector, who have in the past, are now, or may in the future be subjected to the policies, practices and conduct of INS and/or the Border Patrol during the course of INS area control operations directed at places of employment."

It therefore follows that a class may properly consist of "All persons of African ancestry, who have been stopped, detained, questioned or searched by police officials while driving or sitting in a vehicle on a public roadway within the Toronto Region."

COMMON ISSUES

The underlying consideration is a determination of whether a class proceeding will avoid duplication of fact-finding or legal analysis. An issue will, therefore, be common only where its resolution is necessary to the resolution of each class member's claim and an issue will not be "common" unless it is a substantial ingredient of each of the class member's claims.
Reference: Hollick v. Metropolitan Toronto (Municipality) (2001), 13 C.P.C. (5th) 1 (S.C.C.) (class action based on claim of environmental damage suffered by property owners located near large garbage dump; some aspects of issue of liability common to all members, such as showing defendant emitting pollutants; even though complaints higher in some areas, complaints still widespread).

However, the fact that an assessment of damages is required for each member of the class does not prevent the finding that there are common issues. Reference: Delgrosso v. Paul (1999), 41 C.P.C. (4th) 390 (Ont. Gen. Div.); leave to appeal refused (1999), 46 C.P.C. (4th) 140 (Ont. Div. Ct.) (class proceedings sought for approximately 150 investors in syndicated mortgage transactions; important common issue whether defendant lawyer owed duty to investors as opposed to trustees of syndicate; individual assessment of damages would not detract from common issues); Nantais v. Telectronics Proprietary (Canada) Ltd. (1995), 40 C.P.C. (3d) 245 (Ont. Gen. Div.); leave to appeal refused (1995), 40 C.P.C. (3d) 263 (Ont. Gen. Div.) (class action commenced on behalf of persons implanted with certain leads for pacemakers; plaintiffs proposing certification only for determination of liability; common issue was whether defendant was negligent in manufacture, design and distribution of product which was sufficient even though many individual factual issues existed, such as different patients and doctors).

It would appear from a review of case-law in the United States that the issue of commonality in relation to racial profiling cases poses some potential problems. As a general rule, it would appear that the police officials must have acted in terms of a standard policy or practice of the organ of state before commonality can be found. Indeed, there would be no commonality if each police official acted out his own bias or prejudice, rather than in terms of a standard policy or procedure.

In this regard, in White v. Williams 208 F.R.D. 123 it was found that the proposed class of "[a]ll persons of color who were stopped, detained, and/or searched by New Jersey State Police on the New Jersey Turnpike for the period January 1, 1993 through April 3, 2001" was overly broad, and thus could not be certified in action alleging that state officials violated African–American motorists' civil rights through conducting, endorsing and covering up state police's practice of racial profiling. The definition involved several State Police Superintendents and three administrations, included no geographic distinctions, and did not attempt to distinguish between persons who were breaking traffic law when they were stopped and those who were not. Furthermore, common issues did not predominate issues unique to individual class members' claims and thus class certification was not appropriate on ground that class action was superior to traditional forms of litigation, even if officials acted in common and consistent manner with respect to all class members because individual determinations would have had to be made in order to determine whether discriminatory intent motivated stop of each class member, whether each class member was issued citation, and whether each citation was valid.

The following cases also took a similar approach:
Rodriguez v. National City Bank, No. 08-2059, 2011 U.S. Dist. LEXIS 101367 (E.D. Pa. Sept. 8, 2011) (Robreno, J.) (denying plaintiffs' motion for certification of settlement class where plaintiffs alleged that bank discriminated against minority home loan applicants; no commonality where many loan officers used their own discretion to perpetrate the alleged discrimination).

Bennett v. Nucor Corp., Nos. 09-3831/3834 and 10-1332, 2011 U.S. App. LEXIS 19395 (8th Cir. Sept. 22, 2011) (affirming denial of class certification in action alleging racial discrimination under disparate treatment and disparate impact liability theories; commonality not satisfied where employment practices varied substantially in each department and where defendant's management was decentralized and each department was autonomous).

Ellis v. Costco Wholesale Corp., No. 07-15838, 2011 U.S. App. LEXIS 19060 (9th Cir. Sept. 16, 2011) (vacating and remanding the district court's certification of class where plaintiffs alleged that Costco engaged in gender discrimination when promoting employees; district court failed to engage in the "rigorous analysis" mandated by Wal-Mart to determine whether "there was significant proof that [Costco] operated under a general policy of discrimination").

In contrast, however, where reliance was placed on a policy, rather than a practice perpetuated by individual perpetrators within the scope of their employment, certification has been granted.

For example, in in Ortega-Melendres v. Arpaio 836 F.Supp.2d 959 (2011) the court certified as a class "All Latino persons who, since January, 2007, have been or will be in the future, stopped, detained, questioned or searched by MCSO agents while driving or sitting in a vehicle on a public roadway or parking area in Maricopa County, Arizona."

The court reasoned as follows on the issue of commonality:

"To satisfy the commonality prong, class members

need not allege that they "have all suffered a violation of the same provision of law," but their claims "must depend upon a common contention — for example, the assertion of discriminatory bias on the part of the same supervisor." Wal-Mart Stores, Inc. v. Dukes, ___ U.S. ___, 131 S.Ct. 2541, 2551, 180 L.Ed.2d 374 (2011). Although the factual circumstances of the individual stops involving the named Plaintiffs differ, they claim generally that MCSO has a policy of racial profiling, in violation of the Fourteenth Amendment, which leads officers to detain individuals without reasonable suspicion that they committed a crime, in violation of the Fourth Amendment. (Doc. 26 ¶ 2-4). In a civil rights suit, "commonality is satisfied where the lawsuit challenges a system-wide practice or policy that affects all of the putative class members." Armstrong v. Davis, 275 F.3d 849, 868 (9th Cir.2001), abrogated on other grounds by Johnson v. California, 543 U.S. 499, 125 S.Ct. 1141, 160 L.Ed.2d 949 (2005) (citing LaDuke, 762 F.2d at 1332). As other courts have noted, commonality in cases alleging racial profiling is satisfied when "the injuries complained of by the named plaintiffs allegedly resulted from the same unconstitutional practice or policy that allegedly injured or will injure the proposed class members."Daniels v.

City of New York, 198 F.R.D. 409, 418 (S.D.N.Y.2001).

Likewise, differences in the subjective motivations between MCSO officers conducting stops does not defeat typicality of claims alleging a departmental policy of violating constitutional rights, whether under the Fourth or the Fourteenth Amendments. "In assessing typicality, the court considers `the nature of the claim or defense of the class representative, and not the specific facts from which it arose or the relief sought." Winkler v. DTE, Inc., 205 F.R.D. 235, 241"

Likewise, in International Molders' and Allied Workers' Local Union No. 164 v. Nelson, 102 F.R.D. 457, 38 Fed.R.Serv.2d 1125, the certified class was described as "all persons of Hispanic or other Latin American ancestry, residing or working within the jurisdiction of the San Francisco District Office of the United States Immigration and Naturalization Service (INS) and/or the Livermore Border Patrol Sector, who have in the past, are now, or may in the future be subjected to the policies, practices and conduct of INS and/or the Border Patrol during the course of INS area control operations directed at places of employment."

In finding commonality, the court reasoned as follows:

"Commonality Requirement Rule 23(a)(2) requires that there be questions of law or fact common to the class before the action may proceed as a class action. The commonality requirement does not mean that all questions of law and fact must be common to class members, *462 Jordan v. County of Los Angeles, 669 F.2d at 1320, but rather, the commonality requirement can be found to be met where only one of many issues of law or fact is common to all class members. Blackie v. Barrack, 524 F.2d 891, 904 (9th Cir.1975), cert. denied, 429 U.S. 816, 97 S.Ct. 57, 50 L.Ed.2d 75 (1976); Wilcox Development Co. v. First Interstate Bank of Oregon, 97 F.R.D. 440, 443 (D.Or.1983).

In the present case common issues of fact include: whether persons are detained and interrogated solely or primarily because of their Hispanic or Latin ancestry; whether defendants coerce persons to waive their constitutional rights; and, whether defendants surround business premises without cause. Common questions of law include: whether defendants can surround or secure business premises without reasonable suspicion that the persons inside are illegal aliens; whether defendants can enter business premises without a legally sufficient warrant or consent; whether defendants can approach, detain and interrogate employees solely because of their Hispanic or Latin American ancestry; and, whether defendants must advise the employees of their constitutional rights before detaining and interrogating them.

Defendants assert that the commonality requirement is not met with respect to the proposed plaintiff class because analysis and proof unique to each individual class member will be required to resolve the merits of plaintiffs' lawsuit. Defendants have two bases for this assertion. First, defendants contend that constitutional rights are personal. Second, defendants contend that whether each class member's constitutional rights were violated is dependent upon individual items of proof such as the class member's appearance and conduct during the raid, whether the raid was pursuant to a warrant or consent, and whether the INS agents had articulable facts which led to the questioning and detention of each class member.

Where a class action is sought to be maintained pursuant to subsection (b)(2) of Rule 23, which authorizes a class action where the party opposing the class has acted on grounds generally applicable to the class thereby making injunctive and declaratory relief appropriate,FN1 the personal character of constitutional rights is not a proper basis for negating the commonality, or any other, requirement for maintenance of a class action. Subsection (b)(2) was designed largely to permit maintenance of a class action as a vehicle for the redress of civil rights violations. Alliance to End Repression v. Rochford, 565 F.2d 975, 979, n. 9 (7th Cir.1977). To accept defendants' argument that the personal nature of constitutional rights precludes a finding of commonality would put an end to class litigation concerning deprivations of civil rights, a result that was clearly not intended by the draftees of Rule 23 and a result which cannot be countenanced by this Court. See Id.

Defendants' contention that the commonality requirement is not satisfied because individual items of proof will arise in determining the merits of each class member's claim is without merit for two reasons. First, as previously discussed, the commonality requirement will be found to be met when as few as one common issue of law or fact is present among members of the proposed class. See, e.g., Blackie v. Barrack, 524 F.2d at 904. In the present case, as the Court earlier set forth, there are numerous questions of law and fact common to the proposed plaintiff class. Second, even though individual factual circumstances may be present among class members, the commonality requirement is satisfied where it is alleged that the defendants have acted in a uniform manner with respect to the class. Alliance to End Repression, 565 F.2d at 979; Midwest Community Counsel v. Chicago Park District, 87 F.R.D. 457, 462 (E.D.Ill.1980). In the present case plaintiffs allege a systematic and uniform practice of the defendants in conducting workplace raids, and allege that these uniform practices are the cause of the deprivation of constitutional*463 rights suffered by the proposed plaintiff class. Thus, sufficient common questions of law and fact are present among class members to permit class litigation of the alleged constitutional deprivations.

Although there may be some legitimate individual factual differences among members of the proposed class, these issues are largely insignificant in resolving the class portion of the complaint in light of the fact that damages are not sought by the proposed class, and in light of the numerous important common issues of law and fact raised by the class portion of the complaint.
Accordingly, under the relatively relaxed standards in the Ninth Circuit for a finding of commonality, see, e.g., Blackie v. Barrack, 524

F.2d at 904, the Court finds that the commonality requirement of Rule 23(a)(2) is satisfied."

And finally, in Morrow v. City of Tenaha Deputy City Marshall Washington, No. 2-08-cv-288, 2011 U.S. Dist. LEXIS 96829 (E.D. Tex. Aug. 29, 2011) the court certified a class iaction alleging that city officials developed a discriminatory traffic stop practice that targeted racial minorities. The court reasoned that the commonality requirement was satisfied where a small and centralized group of city officials conceived and implemented interdiction policy and the plaintiffs had significant proof of a "general policy of discrimination" given the plaintiffs' proffered statistics and anecdotes and the fact that city failed to maintain racial profiling information as required by Texas law.

It therefore follows that to the extent that there is evidence of a policy or practice of racial profiling or discrimination, the commonality test will met and certification will likely be granted.

Preferable Procedure For Resolution of Common Issues

Before a class proceeding can be certified, the fourth requirement is that a class proceeding would be a preferable procedure for the resolution of the common issues.
Reference: Class Proceedings Act, 1992, S.O. 1992, c. 6, s. 5(1).

And, in the absence of legislative guidelines as to what would be the preferable procedure for the resolution of the common issues, the issue should be decided by reference to the three principal advantages of class actions: judicial economy, access to justice and behaviour modification.

Reference: Hollick v. Metropolitan Toronto (Municipality) (2001), 13 C.P.C. (5th) 1 (S.C.C.) (class proceeding not preferable procedure as common issues negligible in comparison to individual claims; small claims trust fund already set up by defendant to satisfy claims and environmental legislation made behavioural modification of class action less important); Abdool v. Anaheim Management Ltd. (1995), 31 C.P.C. (3d) 197 (Ont. Div. Ct.) (plaintiffs purchasing condominiums as tax-sheltered investment; project failing; plaintiffs suing developer, developer's solicitors, trust company which financed project, real estate brokers and accounting firm; action based on allegations of misrepresentation as to financial arrangements and financial projections; plaintiffs' motion for certification dismissed; class action not preferred procedure);Carom v. Bre-X Minerals Ltd. (2000), 1 C.P.C. (5th) 62 (Ont. C.A.); leave to appeal refused (2001), 283 N.R. 399 (note) (S.C.C.); Nantais v. Telectronics Proprietary (Canada) Ltd. (1995), 40 C.P.C. (3d) 245 (Ont. Gen. Div.); leave to appeal refused (1995), 40 C.P.C. (3d) 263 (Ont. Gen. Div.) (class action commenced on behalf of persons implanted with certain leads for pacemakers; plaintiffs proposing certification only for determination of liability; class action was preferable procedure as only procedure by which such a costly claim could be brought to trial by spreading out cost over many plaintiffs); Robertson v. Thomson Corp.(1999), 30 C.P.C. (4th) 182 (Ont. Gen. Div.) (all three goals for class actions as preferable procedure met when thousands of small claims by numerous writers alleged misuse of copyright by publisher; certified as class proceeding); Chadha v. Bayer Inc. (2001), 8 C.P.C. (5th) 138 (Ont. Div. Ct.); affirmed (2003), 2003 CarswellOnt 49 (Ont. C.A.); leave to appeal refused (2003), 2003 CarswellOnt 2810 (S.C.C.) (proposed class action by homeowners regarding price-fixing with respect to ingredients manufactured by defendants not providing judicial economy; Competition Bureau could provide behaviour modification); Knowles v. Wyeth-Ayerst Canada Inc. (2001), 16 C.P.C. (5th) 330 (Ont. S.C.J.); additional reasons at (2001), 16 C.P.C. (5th) 341 (Ont. S.C.J.) (action involving complex medical issues; unduly expensive and difficult for individuals to pursue claims individually); Markson v. MBNA Canada Bank (2007), 2007 CarswellOnt 2716(Ont. C.A.); leave to appeal refused (2007), 2007 CarswellOnt 7420 (S.C.C.) (criteria for preferable procedure includes consideration of judicial economy, access to justice and behaviour modification; class proceeding not only preferable procedure, but only viable procedure for remedying alleged wrong and calling alleged wrongdoer into account).

Further, when considering whether a class proceeding is the proper procedure, the court must also consider whether a class proceeding is a fair, efficient and manageable way of advancing the claim such that a determination of the common issues will advance the litigation in a fair, efficient and manageable way.

Reference: Williams v. Mutual Life Assurance Co. of Canada (2000), 24 C.C.L.I. (3d) 298 (Ont.

S.C.J.) (proposed class proceeding concerning premiums for life insurance policies; class action not certified as unknown number of class members, many unidentifiable, each signing individual contracts of varying terms).

In the present matter, the author will merely refer to one (1) case to demonstrate why proceeding by means of class action is appropriate. In International Molders' and Allied Workers' Local Union No. 164 v. Nelson, 102 F.R.D. 457, 38 Fed.R.Serv.2d 1125, the court noted as follows:

"Discovery conducted in this case has revealed that at least 456 persons of Mexican or Latin American heritage were detained and questioned during the raids conducted thus far by defendants. Joinder of 456 persons as plaintiffs to this action would be extremely inconvenient, as it would be expensive and burdensome to the parties, and it would create massive organizational problems for the Court. See Harris v. Palm Springs Alpine Estates, 329 F.2d at 913; In re Itel Securities Litigation, 89 F.R.D. 104, 112 (N.D.Cal.1981); In re Gap Stores Litigation, 79 F.R.D. 283, 302 (N.D.Cal.1978). Additionally, the proposed class includes unknown and unnamed future members, making a conclusion that joinder is impracticable particularly compelling. Jordan v. County of Los

Angeles, 669 F.2d 1311, 1320 (9th Cir.1982), judgment vacated on other grounds, 459 U.S. 810, 103 S.Ct. 35, 74 L.Ed.2d 48 (1982). Class litigation of this lawsuit is highly desirable."

In precisely the same way, joinder is entirely impractical in the present matter,, and would be expensive and burdensome in light of the number of persons who would need to be jointed as plaintiffs. And furthermore, behaviour modification is best served through class proceedings, rather than individual claims.

The author therefore feels that class proceedings are the preferable method to resolve this matter.

REPRESENTATIVE PLAINTIFF

It has been held that "Representation is adequate when named plaintiffs will pursue the action vigorously on behalf of the class and when they have no conflicts of interest with other class members."

Reference: Ortega-Melendres v. Arpaio 836 F.Supp.2d 959 (2011).

There is no reason to doubt this is the case in the present matter, and therefore, the author will not discuss this any further.

CONCLUSION

In summary, the requirements to certify a class proceeding are that (a) the pleadings or the notice of application discloses a cause of action; (b) there is an identifiable class of two or more persons that would be represented by the representative plaintiff or defendant; (c) the claims or defences of the class members raise common issues; (d) a class proceeding would be the preferable procedure for the resolution of the common issues; and (e) there is a representative plaintiff or defendant.

In the present matter, the only potential area of dispute would relate to the existence of common issues (or commonality). However, if reliance is placed on a standard practice, common issues will likely be demonstrated.

CHAPTER
8

A LETTER TO THE JUDICIAL AND POLITICAL ESTABLISHMENTS TO ABOLISH RACIAL PROFILING, (2010)

Dr. MunyonzweHamalengwa
(July 10th, 2010)

The Right Hon. Prime Minister
Mr. Stephen Harper
Prime Minister of Canada
House of Commons
80 rue Wellington Street
Ottawa, ON, K1A 0A2

The Right Hon. Chief Justice
Madam Beverley McLachlin
Supreme Court Building
Ottawa, ON, K1A 0J1

The Right Hon. Premier of Ontario
Mr. Dalton McGuinty,
Legislative Building
Queen's Park
Toronto, ON, M7A 1A1

Toronto Police Chief
Mr. Bill Blair
40 College Street
Toronto, ON, M5G 2J3

Office of the Ombudsman of Ontario
Mr. André Marin
Bell Trinity Square
483 Bay Street, 10th Floor, South Tower
Toronto, ON, M5G 2C9

Minister of Justice and Attorney
General of Canada
The Hon. Rob Nicholson, P.C., Q.C.,
284 Wellington Street
Ottawa, Ontario K1A 0H8

The Chief Justice of Ontario

The Hon. Warren K. Winkler
130 Queen Street West
Toronto, ON, M5H 2N6

Chief Justice of the Superior Court of Justice
The Hon. Heather J. Smith
130 Queen Street West
Toronto, ON, M5H 2N6

The Attorney General of Ontario
Mr. Chris Bentley
720 Bay Street, 8th Floor
Toronto, ON, M5G 2K1

The Toronto Police Service Board
Dr. Alok Mukherjee
40 College Street
Toronto, ON, M5G 2J3

Your Honourables and Gentlemen:

Re: Equity, Equality and Racial Profiling in Canada

Please find enclosed a document addressed to and prepared for you on the above-noted topic. I am submitting it to you for your action to stem the documented practice of Racial Profiling against

African-Canadians and other racial, ethnic and Aboriginal minorities in Canada.

Racially profiled individuals cannot be said to be benefiting from the equal application and benefit of the law as mandated by sections 15 and 27 of the *Canadian Charter of Rightsand Freedoms*. Individual litigation against Racial Profiling has proven futile. In fact, this strategy has hidden more than it has exposed the practice. The Judiciary does not contextualise individual litigation. Law enforcement agencies deny the existence of Racial Profiling even while it is exposed to be existing.

Racial Profiling requires the intervention of political action by our elected representatives as well as judicial and law enforcement agencies' participation in its resolution. In other words, joint-action is required of the Federal and Provincial governments, the Judiciary and the law enforcement agencies.

Political intervention is derived from Sections 91(27) and 92(14) and (15), respectively, of the *Constitution Act*, 1867; Section 15 of the *Charter* and the *Universal Declaration of Human Rights*; the *International Covenant on Civil and Political Rights*; the *International Convention on the*

Elimination of All Forms of Racial Discrimination; and other national and international laws.

Judicial intervention is derived from the courts' traditional jurisdiction as the protectors of the vulnerable, the minorities, the powerless, and the marginalised, and from various human rights laws and sections 15, 24 and 27 of the *Charter*, among others.

Law enforcement agencies derive their responsibilities and obligations to prevent Racial Profiling from the *Police Service Act*, sections 15 and 27 of the *Charter*, human rights codes, and etcetera.

The Ombudsman is empowered to investigate wrong doing or perceived wrong doing, etcetera, by government agencies.

I am requesting a coordinated effort from and by you to initiate a National Commission of Inquiry into Equality Under the Law and the Combating of the Practice of Racial Profiling in Canada.
Thank you for considering this matter,

Yours truly,
Munyonzwe Hamalengwa

An Argument for Equity and Equality in the Application and Enforcement of the Law: The Need for Governmental, Judicial and Law Enforcement Agencies' Involvement in the Battles against Racial Profiling in Canada

Discussion Paper Aimed at Igniting Reform Initiatives Submitted and Presented to the Prime Minister of Canada; Minister of Justice for Canada; Chief Justice of the Supreme Court of Canada; The Premier of Ontario; The Attorney General of Ontario; The Chief Justice of Ontario; The Toronto Police Services Board; The Toronto Police Chief; and the Ombudsman for Ontario.

This submission presents evidence of the existence of racial profiling in Canada and especially in Toronto, Ontario.

It is submitted that the issue of racial profiling has reached gigantic proportions and mandates governmental and judicial intervention from the Prime Minister and the Chief Justice of Canada all the way down to the cop on the beat.

VIOLATION OF CHARTER RIGHTS

Section 15 of the *Charter* states: "(1) Every individual is equal before and under the law and has the right to the equal protection and equal benefit of the law without discrimination and, in particular, without discrimination based on race, national or ethnic origin, colour, religion, sex, age or mental or physical disability. (2) Subsection (1) does not preclude any law, program or activity that has as its object the amelioration of conditions of disadvantaged individuals or groups including those that are disadvantaged because of race, national or ethnic origin, colour, religion, sex, age or mental or physical disability."

Racial profiling also engages sections 7, 8, 9 and 12 of the *Charter*.

Section 7 of the *Charter* reads: "Everyone has the right to life, liberty and security of the person and the right not to be deprived thereof except in accordance with the principles of fundamental justice."

DENIAL OF EQUALITY/RACIAL PROFILING

Racial profiling is generally denied as existing. "Denial of Equality/Racial profiling" refers to the practice whereby law enforcement personnel and others either consciously or unconsciously deny certain segments of society, the equal protection and benefit of the law as is guaranteed by section 15 of the *Charter*. In other words this practice is an unwritten and an unsanctioned form of discrimination.

Those who engage in racial profiling employ a pattern and practice of denial of equality and/or racial profiling in dealing with the victims and /or fail to prevent, address or end the notorious issue of denial of equality/racial profiling.
The victims find that the acts and omissions of the perpetrators of racial profiling violate their rights to security of the person and the right not to be deprived thereof except in accordance with the principles of fundamental justice and are denied their equality rights as guaranteed respectively by sections 7 and 15 of *Canadian Charter of Rights and Freedoms*.

The existence of racial profiling has been proven by the following studies among others:

The 2005 Kingston Data Collection Project

In 2005 the Kingston Police inaugurated the Kingston Data Collection Project following an incident which happened in 2001 in which several Black youths were involved. They had police firearms drawn on them, but were found to have not been engaged in any wrongdoing. In 2003 two teenagers were involved in no wrongdoing, but one of the Black youths had also been involved in the 2001 incident. From October 1, 2003 until midnight on September 30, 2004, the Kingston police officers were asked to collect data whenever they interacted with citizens in a non-casual manner. This meant that when a Kingston officer interrogated, suspected, searched, warned, charged, or completed a police computer check on a person, whether on the street or in a vehicle, race and ethnicity data were to be collected. It was found that racially biased policing occurred and occurs when law enforcement inappropriately considers race or ethnicity in deciding with whom and how to intervene in an enforcement capacity.

A study of police statistics in Kingston, Ontario, released in May 2005 found that young Black and aboriginal men were more likely to be stopped than other groups. The data showed that police in the predominantly White city were 3.7 times more likely to stop a Black as a Caucasian, and 1.4 times more likely to stop an aboriginal person than a White. Racial profiling takes away the Black or Aboriginal people's fundamental human freedoms.

2002 *Toronto Star* Analysis of Toronto Police Statistics

In 2002, the *Toronto Star* analyzed Police statistics. From the arrest data gathered by the Police force itself from 1996 to 2002, the analysis found that Blacks charged with simple drug possession were taken to a police station more often than Whites facing the same charge. Once at the station, twice as many Black suspects were held overnight for bail as Whites.

From the same 2002 analysis on traffic offences, the report showed that a disproportionate number of Blacks received tickets for non-moving traffic offences.

In a *Toronto Star* article of October 19, 2002, titled "Singled out: Star analysis of police crime data shows justice is different for Blacks and Whites" it is reported thatBlacks arrested by Toronto Police are treated more harshly than Whites. Black people, charged with simple drug possession, are taken to police stations more often than Whites facing the same charge. Once at the station, accused Blacks are held overnight, for a bail hearing, at twice the rate of Whites.

The Toronto crime data also shows a disproportionate number of Black motorists are ticketed for violations that only surface following a traffic stop. This difference, say civil libertarians, community leaders and criminologists, suggests police use racial profiling in deciding whom to pull over.

The evidence is contained in a massive police database recording more than 480,000 incidents in which an individual was arrested, or ticketed, for an offence dating back to 1996. It included almost 800,000 criminal and other charges which the Star obtained through a freedom of information request, marking the first time access to these numbers was granted to anyone outside the police community.

Police are forbidden, by their governing board, from analyzing this data in terms of race. The findings provide hard evidence of what Blacks have long suspected - race matters in Canadian society especially when dealing with police.

Elementary school teacher Robinson wanted to be a police officer when he was younger. In 2003, he gave anonymous testimony in the human rights inquiry into racial profiling regarding 10 encounters he had had with Toronto police between 2000 and 2002, in which he believed his skin colour was a factor. Out of the 10 incidents, nine involved traffic stops and most resulted in no ticket. He was in his mid-20s then. The *Star* tracked Robinson down at Oakridge Junior Public School to see what's changed for him. He's just bought a house, is working on a master's thesis and is coaching both the boys' and girls' school basketball teams. He also recently wrote a paper on student perspectives on having police officers in their schools. The number of times he's been pulled over by police since he testified? He smiles and says he's lost count. About 20, he guesses. He does not have a criminal record. Robinson is an example of Black school children who have escaped racial profiling. Others, however, may not be lucky like Robinson. The result is that more and more Black children may fail to complete school and be useful citizens due to racial profiling.

Royson James, columnist at the *Toronto Star* wrote of how racial profiling affects his own family: "Only some of us parents know the palpable, paralyzing fear that the car will be stopped by Toronto, Peel, Durham or York police, searched, have its passengers harassed and humiliated - simply because the driver is our Black son."

"A significant number of police officers feel Blacks are criminal beasts deserving attention from law enforcers; that some elements of society harbour such racist sentiments; that Black don't have the same freedom to make mistakes like everyone else because the consequences could be harsher, the punishment more severe" wrote Royson James on "Why I Fear For My Sons." In the *Toronto Star* on October 21, 2002.

Recent *Toronto Star* Analysis of Toronto Police Statistics (2010 Studies)

In an article published by the *Toronto Star* on February 11, 2010 : "Racial profiling still has no place here" data analyzed about who Toronto police stopped between 2003 and 2008, results show that Black and brown youth are 2.5 times more likely to be stopped than White youth.

On February 6, 2010 the *Toronto Star* reported a stark Racial Profiling reality from the data collected from the Police under the freedom of information request that spanned nearly seven years. It is titled: “Race Matters: Blacks documented by police at high rate.”

The data found that the Toronto Police question Black people at a disproportionately high rate. Skin colour is identified in the police data as being either "White," "Black," "Brown," or "Other." This is based on officer assessments. The data comes from three source databases and details incidents and stops from the beginning of 2003 to the end of 2008. Two of the datasets relate to police contact cards, and the third is data on arrests and charges. Police removed names and other identifying elements from the data.
Further, the *Star* analysis shows race, age and gender are big factors in who gets stopped. Looking at Blacks and Whites of all ages, Blacks are three times more likely to be stopped.

Male Blacks aged 15-24 are stopped and documented 2.5 times more than White males the same age.

The *Star* analysis of Police Carding, a process of filling out a 208 card of information on any individual, revealed a disparity in who is carded, with Blacks being carded more than Whites.

Differences between Black and White carding rates are highest in more affluent, mostly White areas of the city, such as North Toronto and the Kingsway, the *Star* found. Criminologist Wortley calls this the “out-of-place” phenomenon. It’s a natural thing to expect from officers on the lookout of for things unusual or different, says Wortley, who oversaw a police stop data-collection pilot project by Kingston police.

Although Blacks make up 8.4 per cent of Toronto’s population, they account for three times as many contact cards. The collateral damage is law-abiding civilians who feel they are being treated unfairly because they are Black.

In the *Toronto Star* articles titled: “Racial bias exists on police force, chief says” of September 30, 2009, Police Chief, Bill Blair, acknowledged that racial profiling is a problem in Ontario: "Racism is a human failing. Racial profiling can occur. We've acknowledged that right upfront and that has really enabled us to work with our community partners to do something about it."

In each of the city’s 74 police patrol zones, the *Star* analysis shows that Blacks were documented at significantly higher rates than their overall census population by zone. “It doesn’t matter what type of neighbourhood you live in or what type of neighbourhood you're travelling through, if you are Black you are much more likely to attract the attention of the police and therefore have a contact card filled out," says University of Toronto criminologist Scot Wortley, who reviewed the *Star* analysis.

Robinson, who wears his hair in short dreads, is troubled by this. And he's far from alone. Max Rose, 16, who is regularly questioned by police in the Jane and Finch-area building he lives in, says he feels embarrassed when neighbour gather to watch.

Kasim St. Remy, 14, was recently stopped and questioned by police. He hadn't done anything wrong. This bothers his mother, Clemee Joseph: "It is hard for me when the police stop him to question him and have him on their radar. I know that my son is a good kid."

In May, 2009, Jarvis St. Remy, 18, was killed in what is believed to be case of mistaken identity. St. Remy had no history with police, who have yet to make an arrest. "I don't like the stereotyping of this ... they get the good kids and the bad kids all in one," Joseph says. "But that is what is happening with the Black kids, so that's who they have to stop."

In the *Toronto Star* article of July 21, 2008, titled: "Is justice system blind to colour?" visible minorities charged with a crime in Canada are less likely to be convicted, but more likely to have a DNA sample taken. They're also more likely to have police warnings on their file for violence, escape risk and suicidal behaviour. These differences were identified in a *Star* analysis of the criminal histories of nearly 3 million people. The data comes from the Canadian Police Information Centre (CPIC) database, in which race is recorded as White or non-White. The data obtained by the *Star* contains two kinds of files: 2.4 million criminal records where a conviction was registered and 500,000 criminal histories, where there was a charge but no conviction.

The *Star*'s analysis of the data shows that non-Whites were 53 per cent more likely than Whites not to be convicted. One explanation for the difference is that judges could be giving more discharges to non-White offenders as a "reward" for dead time spent in jail awaiting trial. The 1995 Report of the Commission on Systemic Racism in the Ontario Criminal Justice System determined that Black accused, for example, are more often held without bail than their White counterparts.

The *Star* analysis of CPIC data shows that 32.5 per cent of those required to provide DNA samples were non-White, even though non-Whites make up only 16.7 per cent of those with criminal records.

The difference in who gives samples cannot be explained simply by differences in the seriousness of charges. (Non-Whites account for a disproportionately high 23.9 per cent of records for violent offences; the same for robbery.)

Comparing the same kinds of criminal records still shows a difference between Whites and non-Whites. For example, of people who have a criminal record for violence, 10.5 per cent of non-Whites had DNA taken versus 6.1 per cent of Whites.

With a record for robbery (and nothing else) non-Whites are 50 per cent more likely to have had a sample taken.

Non-Whites are more likely to have warnings on their file than Whites indicating they are considered violent or a suicide risk. These, along with notations for mental instability and escape risk, are entered by local police forces. The differences remain even when looking at Whites and non-Whites with similar records. For example, of those with criminal records for violent offences, non-Whites are more likely to also have a notation for violent behaviour marked on their record.

On September 30, 2009 Police Chief Blair is quoted in the *Toronto Star* as having admitted that racial profiling exits in Toronto: "Racism is a human failing. Racial profiling can occur. We've acknowledged that right upfront and that has really enabled us to work with our community partners to do something about it," said Blair. Blair said nine out of 10 youths stopped and documented on a street corner may be perfectly good kids, and the encounter might leave them “pissed at us.” Racial profiling clearly contributes to Black youths’ view of the police as racists.

The *Star* analysis shows police begin documenting youth in certain “at-risk” neighbourhoods in serious numbers when they are on the cusp of becoming teenagers. The carding peaks in the late teens and gradually diminishes as people reach their 30s and 40s. This leads to the Black youth being perceived as troubled-kids.

"Regardless of intentions, police questioning can be intimidating and coercive," writes Des Rosiers. "When perceived as excessive of discriminatory, it can create distrust in law enforcement, undermine public faith in police, and, ultimately, weaken efforts to root out and punish crime."

Racial profiling affects the visible minority in employment. In the Police force in 2008 only 51 of 332 recruits - or 15 per cent of the total new hirings - represented visible minorities in one of the world's most multicultural cities. In 2009, only 11 per cent of the class is a visible minority. The force could not tell the *Star* how many of those recruits are Black. Nor could it say how many Black officers are currently on staff.

Thomas, who works in the pro bono office of the Law Society of Upper Canada, said a deep-rooted police subculture poses a barrier to minority officers. "If you want to push Black issues you won't get promoted. And the (Black officers) who do get promoted are basically promoted because they buy into the police subculture."

The Canada Race Relations Foundation

The Canada Race Relations Foundation reported the prevalence and impact of racial profiling in the workplace. There is ample evidence to indicate the occurrence and negative effects of racial profiling both at the workplace and at places of community integration where security and policing is required. The ways in which these policies have been and continue to be enforced are harmful to minority communities, perpetuating popular stereotypes and widening the divide between majority and minority communities. There is a need for public education, cultural awareness, cultural sensitivity and the development and implementation of clear and consistent policies to educate and address the conduct of security workers, legislators, and the general public to address the problem of racial profiling.

Racial Profiling Statistics from York University

The study of the crime data carried out by York University revealed significant disparities in the ways in which Blacks and Whites are treated in law enforcement practices. More specifically, the data showed:

A disproportionate number of Black motorists are ticketed for violations that only surface following a traffic stop.
Black people, charged with simple drug possession, are taken to police stations more often than Whites facing the same charge.
Once at the station, accused Blacks are held overnight for a bail hearing at twice the rate of Whites. Clearly these findings show that Black people are discriminated against by the Police force.

Racial profiling is a manifestation of "democratic racism" in which racialized bias and discrimination "cloaks its presence" in liberal principles. Democratic racism is an ideology in which two conflicting sets of values are made congruent to each other. The consequence of this tension ensures that commitments to justice, fairness, and equality conflict but coexist with values and behaviours that include negative feelings about people of colour, and differential treatment of them (Frances Henry & Carol Tator, *Racial Profiling: Challenging the Myth of a "Few Bad Apples"*, 2005)

Accusations of differential treatment arise in areas where authorities can exercise their discretion. If police stopped every car, or if customs officers directed everyone for follow-up scrutiny, there would be no talk of racial profiling. But when that discretion is exercised, members of many minority groups feel that they come out with the short end of the baton – that they somehow always have to prove their innocence. In this regard racial profiling reverses onus on the Black community in which they are presumed guilty until proven innocent.

What does it mean when half the inmates in a provincial jail are aboriginal when they represent only 10 per cent of the community's population? Are aboriginal Canadians committing more crimes or are police simply spending more time in the aboriginal community?

The Ontario Human Rights Commission Report

The Ontario Human Rights Commission Report of December 9, 2003 titled, *Paying the Price: The Human Cost of Racial Profiling* was based on 400 personal accounts of experiences with profiling that individuals shared with the Commission during the course of its Racial Profiling Inquiry held earlier in 2003. The Report looks at the human cost of racial profiling on individuals who have experienced it, their families and their communities and the detrimental impacts of this practice on society as a whole.

"When we launched our inquiry, we found that existing research undertaken both here and in jurisdictions outside Canada provided adequate evidence that racial profiling does occur."

The purpose of the Commission's racial profiling inquiry is twofold: to give a voice to individuals who have experienced profiling, and in doing so, raise awareness of the negative consequences of profiling among people who have not been impacted by it. Ultimately, the Commission hopes to bridge the divide between those who deny the existence of profiling and communities that have long felt that they are being targeted.

The Ontario Human Rights Commission defines racial profiling as any action taken for reasons of safety, security or public protection that relies on stereotypes about race, colour, ethnicity, ancestry, religion or place of origin, rather than on reasonable suspicion.

In a recent survey of Oakville's Black youth aged 13 to 24, researchers were told that adults appear to brand them as troublemakers on the basis of "youthful indiscretions" more quickly than they do White kids doing comparable things. Similarly, they believe adults react differently to White and Black youth wearing the same type of clothing: White kids are assumed to be going through a "phase" while Black youth are more likely to be seen as potential criminals.

Stephen Lewis' 1992 *Report to the Premier on Racism in Ontario* on the issue of police/visible minority relations concluded that visible minorities, particularly African Canadians, experienced discrimination in policing and the criminal justice system. Stephen Lewis recommended that the Task Force on Race Relations and Policing be reconstituted owing to perceived inadequacies with the implementation of the 57 recommendations in its 1989 report. A second report of the Task Force was published in November 1992 which examined the status of the implementation of the recommendations from the 1989 report and offered additional recommendations.

In 1992, the Ontario government also established the Commission on Systemic Racism in the Ontario Criminal Justice System. This Commission studied all facets of criminal justice and in December 1995 issued a 450 page report with recommendations.

The effects of Racial profiling can include:

People are less likely to cooperate with people they mistrust and may develop doubts regarding all aspects of the criminal justice system.

Individuals with these perceptions may respond inappropriately to law enforcement officers out of mistrust or may retaliate for past-perceived injustices. Situations may therefore escalate unnecessarily putting both the citizen and officer at risk of injury.

Safety concerns for officers and community members may be increased in hostile environments.

Left unchecked, mistrust towards the criminal justice system can lead to civil unrest.

It has even been suggested that mistrust of police can be the basis for acquittals in jury trials

Racial profiling targets not only Black criminals, but also deeply impacts on their lives.

The 1995 Report of the Commission on Systematic Racism in the Ontario Criminal Justice System

A major survey conducted in the Metropolitan Toronto found that more than five in ten (58%) Black residents, three in ten (31%) Chinese residents and more than three in ten (36%) White residents believe judges do not treat Black people the same as White people.

More than eight in ten of those who perceive differential treatment believe judges treat Black people worse than White people.

Four in ten (40%) defense counsel and three in ten (33%) provincial division judges appointed since 1989 perceive differential treatment of White and racial minority people in the criminal justice system.

About one in ten Crown attorneys (13%), general division judges (10%) and provincial division judges appointed before 1989 (10%) also perceive unequal treatment by race.

A major study of admissions to Ontario prisons indicates that for the period studied, the majority of prisoners are White, but that Black men, women and male youths are massively over-represented among prison admissions.

The over-representation of Black people reflects a dramatic increase in their admissions to prison between 1986/87 and 1992/93. By the end of those six years, Black adults were admitted to prison at over five times the rate the White adults, disproportionate to their representation in Ontario's population.

The over-representation of Black adults is much worse among those imprisoned before trial than among sentenced admissions. While White people were imprisoned before trial at about the same rate as after sentence (approximately 329 per 100,000 persons in the population before trial, and 334 after sentence), the pre-trial admission rate of Black people was twice their sentenced admission rate (approximately 2,136 per 100,000 before trial, and 1,051 after sentence).

JUDICIAL FINDINGS ON RACIAL PROFILING, RACISIM AND DISCRIMINATION

In the *Parks* decision, the Ontario Court of Appeal stated, "Racism, and in particular anti-black racism, is a part of our community's psyche. A significant segment of our community holds overtly racist views. A much larger segment subconsciously operates on the basis of negative racial stereotypes. Furthermore, our institutions, including the criminal justice system, reflect and perpetuate those negative stereotypes. The criminal trial milieu may also accentuate the role of racial bias in the decision-making process. Anti-black attitudes may connect blacks with crime and acts of violence. A juror with such attitudes who hears evidence describing a black accused as a drug dealer involved in an act of violence may regard his attitudes as having been validated by the evidence. That juror may then readily give effect to his or her preconceived negative attitudes towards blacks without regard to the evidence and legal principles."

In *Pearl*, the Ontario Court of Appeal reiterated this: "The community at large and Courts, in particular, have come, some would say belatedly, to recognize that racism operates in the criminal justice system. With this recognition has come an acceptance by the Courts that racial profiling occurs and is a day-to-day reality in the lives of those minorities affected by it."

In *Golden*, the Supreme Court of Canada accepted the following finding: "The intervener African Canadian Legal Clinic (ACLC) agrees with the appellant that probable cause and warrant requirement should be required for strip searches to be constitutional under s.8 of the Charter. The ACLC says that given the negative stereotyping of African Canadians by police and the large number of African Canadians who are stopped and searched by police, a public process of obtaining a warrant is required to reduce the danger of racist stereotyping by individual police officers, who are more likely than a neutral arbiter to conclude that a strip search of a black person is appropriate. The intervener Aboriginal Legal Services of Toronto (ALST) also advocates a regime of prior authorization for strip searches. We believe it is important to note the submission of the ACLC and the ALST that African Canadians and Aboriginal people are overrepresented in the criminal justice system and are therefore likely to represent a disproportionate number of those who are arrested by police and subjected to person searches, including strip searches (*Report of*

Aboriginal Justice Inquiry of Manitoba (1991), Vol. 1, *The Justice System and Aboriginal People*, at p.107; Cawsey Report, *Justice on Trial: Report of the Task Force on Criminal Justice System and its Impact on the Indian and Métis people of Alberta* (1991), Vol.II,p.7, recommendations 2.48 to 2.50; Royal Commission on Aboriginal peoples, *Bridging the Cultural Divide* (1996), at pp.33-39; Commission on Systematic Racism in the Ontario Criminal Justice System, *Report of the Commission on Systematic Racism in the Ontario Criminal Justice System* (1995)). As a result, it is necessary to develop an appropriate framework governing strip searches in order to prevent unnecessary and unjustified strip searches before they occur."

In *Gladue* the Supreme Court of Canada stated the following: "Aboriginal people are overrepresented in virtually all aspects of the [criminal justice] system. Has this Court...noted in *R. v. Williams*, there is widespread bias against aboriginals people within Canada, and "there is evidence that this widespread racism has translated into systematic discrimination in the criminal justice system." The figures are stark and reflect what may fairly be termed a crisis in the Canadian criminal justice system. The unbalanced ratio of imprisonment for aboriginal offenders flows from a number of sources...[including] bias against aboriginal people and from an unfortunate institutional approach that is more inclined to refuse bail and to impose more and longer prison terms for aboriginal offender."

A Quebec Court judge in *Campbell* found the following: "Socio-economic status is a bifurcated indicator. Young black males are objects of racial profiling if they are well to do and driving expensive cars; they are also the object of racial profiling when they are poor. In this case, no indicators place Alexer Campbell within the economically well to do category."

An Ontario Superior Court of Justice judge asked and answered the following question in *Khan*: "Why did they single out Mr. Khan on Marlee Avenue at about noon on Monday in October and decided to search his car? Because he was a young black male driving an expensive Mercedes. Having concluded that the officers in this case fabricated their evidence in respect of the search of Mr. Khan's car, I cannot find their evidence to be at all reliable with respect to the events leading up to the stop. I accept his evidence that he did nothing to cause the officers to stop him. In any event, even if there had been some minor thing about his driving, I do not believe that was the real reason he was stopped. The police stopped him for an improper purpose. Mr. Khan was targeted for this stop because of racial profiling, because he was a black man with an expensive car."

A judge of the Supreme Court of Canada reasoned in *Ladouceur* albeit in dissent the following: "By contrast, the roving random stop would permit any individual officer to stop any vehicle, at any time, at any place. The decision may be based on any whim. Individual officers will have different reasons. Some may tend to stop younger drivers, others older cars, and so on. Indeed, as pointed out by Tarnopolsky J.A., racial considerations may be a factor too."

In *Ladouceur*another judge stated: "Moreover, the Court's understanding of the implications of the police action may be obscured by the fact that most cases that come before them relate to someone who has already been convicted. The Courts may have little "feel" for what this means to persons who have committed no wrong or any idea of the number of such people who may be harassed by the overly zealous elements in any police force. This case has grave implications for equality in the application of the law. It does not prove but certainly does not detract from this thesis that the appellants in the present case are both members of a visible minority."

The issue is how to prove racial profiling in litigation. The Ontario Court of Appeal in *Brown* laid down the scheme: "A racial profiling claim could rarely be proven by direct evidence. This would involve an admission by a police officer that he or she was influenced by racial stereotypes in the exercise of his or her discretion to stop a motorist. Accordingly, if racial profiling is to be proven it must be done by inference drawn from circumstantial evidence."

REASONED PUBLIC OPINION ON RACIAL PROFILING

Toronto police question hundreds of thousands of people, both walking and driving, every year. In many cases, officers fill out a "208" card, police lingo for an index-card-sized document used as an investigative tool and, according to Chief Bill Blair, a way to "get to know" the neighbourhood. (*Toronto Star*, February 6, 2010)

"I don't like the stereotyping of this ... they get the good kids and the bad kids all in one," Clemee Joseph says. "But that is what is happening with the black kids, so that's who they have to stop." (*Toronto Star*, February 6, 2010)

"Police services, not just in Ontario, but across the country, and to some extent, internationally, are watching with great attention the work that we are doing. There's no question that having chief Blair stand up, you know, to his peers, and acknowledge racial profiling exists within the Toronto Police Service ... gives permission in a sense to other services to acknowledge it," says Barbara Hall, Ontario's Human Rights Chief Commissioner. (*Toronto Star*, February 6, 2010)

"And if it is that kids can't walk to school without having to stop, show their ID and have the officers fill out contact cards, that's heightened surveillance, which is exactly what the essence of racial profiling is all about," says David Tanovich, a University of Windsor law professor and author of *The Colour of Justice: Policing Race in Canada (Toronto Star*, February 6, 2010)

"Regardless of intentions, police questioning can be intimidating and coercive. When perceived as excessive of discriminatory, it can create distrust in law enforcement, undermine public faith in police, and, ultimately, weaken efforts to root out and punish crime," says Canadian Civil Liberties

Association general counsel Nathalie Des Rosiers (*Toronto Star*, February 6, 2010)

Deputy Chief Keith Forde, the city's first black deputy, would like to see the disparity in who is carded shrink away, but he believes black people are carded more often because black people are disproportionately being charged with violent crimes and disproportionately the victims of violent crimes. Seeking out suspects based on witness descriptions in areas where more black people live, he explains, results in more blacks being stopped. "These are things that you cannot dispute," Forde said in an interview. "So, yes, you can see the contact cards being out of proportion. Are we doing something to try and alleviate that? Sure we are. Sure we are." (*Toronto Star*, February 6, 2010)

"Racism is a human failing. Racial profiling can occur. We've acknowledged that right upfront and that has really enabled us to work with our community partners to do something about it. From my own experiences and from what I've seen in society and what's been reported in the media, I think substantial amounts of progress have been made since (the *Star* series). Now does that mean there's no racial profiling or improvements to be made? Not necessarily so," said Blair (*Toronto Star*, September 30, 2009)

“It doesn’t matter what type of neighbourhood you live in or what type of neighbourhood you’re travelling through, if you are black you are much more likely to attract the attention of the police and therefore have a contact card filled out,” says University of Toronto criminologist Scot Wortley, who reviewed the *Star* analysis. (*Toronto Star*, February 6, 2010)

"Some steps were taken at that time, but my sense is that what didn't happen is a very coordinated and systematic effort to deal with the issues that we're now trying to face," says Police Services Board chair Alok Mukherjee. (*Toronto Star*, September 30, 2009)

"My guess," said an Ontario judge who reviewed the findings but who asked not to be identified, "is that if the 'non-whites' have spent more time than 'whites' in pre-trial custody, one of the ways judges may 'reward' them is by giving a discharge rather than registering a conviction, especially as there may be immigration consequences if a conviction is registered." (*Toronto Star*, July 21, 2008)

Defence lawyer Daniel Brown, of the Toronto law firm Pinkofskys, suggests there is over-charging in cases where there are multiple non-white accused. "We see this all the time in large gang projects where hundreds are arrested and thousands of charges are laid, only to see a few accused left at the end of the day facing a handful of charges." (*Toronto Star*, July 21, 2008)

"For whatever reason, the data suggests that minorities are much more likely to be charged without enough evidence for prosecutors to get a conviction. If they are concentrated in particular communities, it could undermine the legitimacy of law enforcement – that the community itself may believe police lay bogus or unwarranted charges as a means of harassment," says David Tanovich (*Toronto Star*, July 21, 2008)

"Analysis of those figures by Star reporters suggested that blacks in Toronto were over-represented in certain offence categories like drug possession and in what were called "out-of-sight" traffic violations, such as driving without a licence. The analysis also suggested that black suspects were more likely to be held in custody for a bail hearing, while white suspects facing similar charges – were more likely to be released at the scene." (*CBC* News Online, May 26, 2005)

"When we launched our inquiry, we found that existing research undertaken both here and in jurisdictions outside Canada provided adequate evidence that racial profiling does occur. Right from the start, I have said that what has been noticeably absent from public discussion on this issue is the effect that racial profiling has on those directly impacted by it, and on Ontario society. The Report is not another statistical study; it focuses on personal experiences of profiling incidents in a number of contexts." (Chief Commissioner Keith Norton of the Ontario Human Rights Commission in a Report entitled "Paying the Price: The Human Cost of Racial Profiling." (December 9, 2009)

"I don't think a day will come, in my lifetime, when I won't be profiled or identified for who I am, and what I am," said Jason Burke, 28. (*Toronto Star*, October 19, 2002*)*

"We found that officers write much more powerful character assassinations of black Defendants than white Defendants," Wortley said. "Things like: 'He's a—hole. He's psychotic. He's a threat to society." (*Toronto Star*, October 19, 2002)

"Most people join the police force to do good work," said Barry Thomas, senior consultant with the

Urban Alliance on Race Relations. "Most police officers are good people; they don't get up in the morning to say, 'Whoa, it's a good day to be a bigot.' "So how is it they end up, every day, having more people of one race in jail than another?" Thomas blames lingering racial stereotypes, and a stubborn police culture that didn't keep pace as Toronto evolved from a staid Anglo community into a world leader in diversity. "(*Toronto Star*, October 19, 2002)

Royson James, columnist at the *Toronto Star* wrote of how racial profiling affects his own family: " only some of us parents know the palpable, paralyzing fear that the car will be stopped by Toronto, Peel, Durham or York police, searched, have its passengers harassed and humiliated - simply because the driver is our black son"(October 21, 2002)

"Profiling is the inverse of law enforcement. In law enforcement, a crime is discovered and the police then look for a suspect who might possibly have committed it. Profiling means that a suspect is discovered and the police then look for a crime for the person to have possibly committed" (Martinot, 2003:168, as quoted inFrances Henry & Carol Tator, *Racial Profiling: Challenging the Myth of a "Few Bad Apples"*)

IMPACT OF RACIAL PROFILING

Racial Profiling "violets human dignity by sending a message to the person that he or she is less worthy of consideration and respect as a human being. The impact of racial profiling on people's dignity and self-esteem was confirmed in almost every submission to the Commission's inquiry." (*Paying the Price: The Human Cost of Racial Profiling*, 2003, p.42)

"Parents, especially described a significant emotional or psychological impact of an incident of profiling experienced by a child, 'As a mother I feel depressed. Every time the phone rings, I believe that it is the school calling to say that my son is in trouble.' Other people indicated that they had not told their families of incidents to protect them of the hurt that it would inflict, 'I never told any of my family. All my family is in Trinidad, the States, England; I did not want to tell them because I didn't want to unnecessarily hurt them because of my experience." (*Paying the Price: The Human Cost of Racial Profiling*, 2003, p.43)

"Many reported being blamed for society's problems or being made to feel like a criminal simply by virtue of race, colour...or ancestry, "These incidents leave me very discouraged as I seem to be lumped in with the bad or criminal element of our society although I know right from wrong and have a determined desire to better myself without breaking the law." (R.R) (*Paying the Price: The Human Cost of Racial Profiling*, 2003, p.44)

"A woman who owns a company was told that she couldn't be the owner of the expensive car she was driving; an African Canadian woman who was paying for a meal at a restaurant had the restaurant employee call the credit card company to see if the card had been reported stolen because the card said "Dr." on it and was being used by an African Canadian woman; a police officer was accused of "impersonating a police officer" when his police badge and identification were found. "All of these individuals felt very demeaned by the assumptions that had been made that because of their skin colour, they could not hold the social status that they do." (*Paying the Price: The Human Cost of Racial Profiling*, 2003, p.44)

"Many people explained that racial profiling caused problems in their relationships with others. Several people reported problems in spousal relationships as a result of racial profiling: "That incident for a couple of hours really stayed with me and I got into kind of a little confrontation with my girlfriend because I was so upset." (R.M) (*Paying the Price: The Human Cost of Racial Profiling*, 2003, p.45)

"In another instance, spousal breakdown was cited as a consequence of racial profiling. The man, who reported losing his job because of racial profiling related to September 11th and consequently suffering depression, indicated that his marriage has broken down as a result." (*Paying the Price: The Human Cost of Racial Profiling*, 2003, p.45)

"Some participants in the inquiry recounted physical effects as a result of their experience of profiling. In some cases, these effects concerned their physical autonomy, dignity and privacy, for example, being strip searched, being frisked, sometimes by officers of the opposite sex, or having intimate body areas searched in public. In other cases, people were made to endure uncomfortable conditions while the incident of profiling occurred such as being made to stand in pouring rain or freezing cold for a long period of time or having a two-year old child sweating in a snowsuit during an excessive delay at Customs." (*Paying the Price: The Human Cost of Racial Profiling*, 2003, p.49)

"Racial profiling also has a very negative impact on the morale of racialized employees. One of the most direct descriptions of an employment-related effect of profiling described during the inquiry came from a man subjected to a racially poisoned work environment, in part due to an incident of racial profiling. While at work, this man, who is African Canadian, and two While co-workers heard a woman from a nearby gas station screaming for help after she had just been robbed. They chased after the culprit, a White man, and the African Canadian man was the one who tackled the perpetrator. By the time they got back, a SWAT team from a police force outside of Toronto was on the scene. The police asked, "Did you catch him?" The manager answered, "Yes", and an officer immediately assumed the African Canadian was the robber and grabbed him by the arm and said, "Come with me." The two White employees involved in the capture were interviewed by the police for witness statements and ultimately received civilian citations while the African Canadian man did not. His employer did not stand up for him and other employees laughed at him because of this incident." (*Paying the Price: The Human Cost of Racial Profiling*, 2003, p.51)

"The Global Business and Economic Roundtable on Addiction and Mental Health has estimated the cost of mental disorders at $11 billion in productivity and $33 billion in total. It is clear that the stress to the individual, caused by racial profiling, forms some part of this cost." (*Paying the Price: The Human Cost of Racial Profiling*, 2003, p.52)

"Profiling may also directly interfere with an employee's ability to carry-out the day-to-day job functions. For example, an employee who travels a lot for work may be impacted by issues of profiling by airport security or Canada customs. One participant who is a professional and travels on business trips outside Canada reported being questioned and delayed several times at borders and airports. He indicated that as a result, he has curtailed business travel." (*Paying the Price: The Human Cost of Racial Profiling*, 2003, p.52)

SIGNIFICANT AUTHORITIES ON RACIAL PROFILING

Professor David M. Tanovich of the Faculty of Law, University of Windsor has demonstrated the existence and the intractability of the phenomenon of racial profiling in his ground breaking book, *The Colour of Justice: Policing Race in Canada*.

Professor Frances Henry and Carol Tator in their numerous publications including their latest, *Racial Profiling: Challenging the Myth of a "Few Bad Apples*", also detail the perversity of racial profiling.

Justice Gary Trotter of the Superior Court of Justice in the book, *The Law of Bail in Canada,* discusses the effects and impact of racial profiling on its targets with negative consequences on the bail process.

POLITICAL AND JUDICIAL INTERVENTION IS MANDATED

Racial profiling has not been systematically addressed and tackled by the political, judicial and law enforcement organs of the Canadian society. A significant segment of the Canadian society is therefore not protected from the ravages of racism and discrimination and is denied the equal application and benefit of the law. Political and judicial intervention to uproot the cancer of racial profiling for the benefit of all Canadians is urgently called for and clearly mandated.

CHAPTER 9

CONCLUSION

Dr. Munyonzwe Hamalengwa

What appears in this book is only a slice of documents and reportage on and of the struggles African Canadians and others, have waged to make their lives and the lives of others better. There is no one struggle answer to all problems of unequal treatment. There are many facets of the struggle. There are also many layers of solutions.
I wish to thank all the participants at the 1994 conference whose transcript forms Chapter 3. I wish to thank most profusely Dr. Nangwaya for agreeing severally to have his excellent study reproduced in this book.

I wish to thank the Board of the Black Action Committee for supporting the publication of this book. I particularly wish to isolate the following persons for special mention: Kingsley Gilliam,

Valarie Steele, Hewitt Loague and Charles Mwewa.

The continuing attacks on African-Canadians are reflected in a symptomatic fashion by the actions of some key players concerning the killing by a white officer of a mentally challenged Black man by the name of Andrew Loku in 2015. The government of Ontario refused to release the name of the officer. The Director of the Special Investigations Unit refused as always, to charge the officer with any criminal offence. He took time to release the report to the attorney general, who in turn sat on it without reading it for a long time despite the fact that it was a hot button issue. The Government of Ontario was faced by demonstrations by the Black Lives Matter movement before it agreed to order for the holding of an inquest into Loku's killing and to conduct an investigative review of the predilections of the Special investigations Unit.

The current proposed legislation on ending carding has been attacked as weak by BADC, the African Canadian Legal Clinic and the Criminal Lawyers Association among other groups. There is not one movement against ending racial profiling in the criminal justice system as a whole. Thus this book is relevant as it deals with a continuing systematic problem of unequal benefit in the application and benefit of the law pertaining to African-Canadians.

The reforms that will ever take place in Canada, particularly Ontario will owe their existence to the selfless sacrifice of Dudley Laws and Charles Roach. There are other people whose recognition will be recorded as the wheels of history roll on. Some of the names of those selfless individuals are contained in chapter 3.

Other people's writings will fill in the gaps that I have left out. This is my small contribution.

- DR. MUNYONZWE HAMALENGWA

ABOUT THE AUTHOR

Dr. Munyonzwe Hamalengwa

"He is a prolific writer and has done considerable work in the area of systemic racism, through his writing and his legal advocacy", so stated The Honorable Sidney B. Linden Commissioner for the Ipperwash Inquiry, May 7, 2004, in reference to Dr. Munyonzwe Hamalengwa.

Born in Zambia, a landlocked Country in South Central Africa, he is the second of four siblings.

Munyonzwe Hamalengwa - in Tonga, his mother's tongue, translates into English as 'Sweet Trouble' , spent his childhood in the eastern part of the agrarian town of Monze, that lies 2.5 hrs from Lusaka the Capital.

His matchless individuality is informed by a wealthy of experiences brought about from the early days when he played with his friends, on red sandy yards of eastern Monze, creating ingenuous toys as well as providing care to his younger siblings while his mother and father planted the nearby farm-land to provide the family with nutritious basic staples. He cherishes his peasant upbringing, calling himself The Village Author.

The teenage stubborn years that followed, full of teen rivalry and rebellion were replaced by years of youthful idealism at the University of Zambia in Lusaka. In 1976 Munyonzwe was detained with other student leaders in solitary confinement in Mumbwa, following demonstrations against the Zambian government's handling of issues related to Angola's Independence and issues of freedom of speech and expression. Seven months later he was released and threatened with banishment to the countryside. He then fled to neighboring Tanzania where he stayed for a year clandestinely studying at the University of Dar Es Salaam because he was not permitted to enrol and study for political reasons. From there he came to Canada in 1977 on a World University Service scholarship.

In Toronto, he studied at York University (1977-79) and later went to the Norman Paterson School of International Affairs at Carleton University (1979-80), Antioch School of Law (now District of Columbia School of Law) in Washington DC(1982-83) and then Osgoode Hall Law School (1986-89). He obtained an LLM in 2001 and a PhD in Law in 2013. While in law school, he served on the Editorial Board of the Osgoode Hall Law Journal. He articled for Ruby and Edwardh, Barristers and solicitors (1989-1990). Dr. Hamalengwa has trained at the following institutions or organizations: The International Institute of Human Rights in Strasbourg, France; International Centre for University Teaching of Human Rights, Strasbourg,; The Hague Academy of International Law; The United Nations in the Modern World in Geneva; The International Labour Organization in Geneva, and The Canadian Human Rights Foundation, Charlottetown, Prince Edward Island.

Dr. Hamalengwa has taught at Carleton University, Seneca College, York University, Nelson Mandela Academy of Applied Legal Studies, Osgoode Hall Law School and School of Law at The Zambian Open University. The courses he has taught include: Legal Process; Criminal Law, International Law; Jurisprudence; Public Law; Police Law; Law and Journalism; Immigration Law; Human Rights Law; The political Economy of Africa; Introduction to the Study of Politics; Introduction to International Relations; State and Revolution in Africa; Urban Economies; African Politics; Sports and Entertainment Law and Scriptural Foundations of the Law. He has held the positions of Co-ordinator for Africa and the Middle East in Washington, DC and Director of African Studies at York University.

Dr. Hamalengwa paracticed Administrative Law, Human Rights Law , Immigration Law, Criminal Law, Constitutional law, and Family law all at both trial and appeal levels and International Law of Human Rights . His zeal for law and justice are influenced by terrible circumstances he endured in his shaping years. His vigorous representation had no subordination to any other interests - ideological, career, personal - but the legitimate interests of the client.

Dr. Hamalengwa has defended all types of cases including murder, arson, drugs, fraud and others. He has also brought novel constitutional challenges that were not popular in Canada at the time including racial profiling in the immigration and criminal law context. His first constitutional case on racial profiling was brought in 1993 (Ritchie et al v.Her Majesty) in Superior Court of Justice. He then did immigration cases on racial profiling some of which went all the way to the Supreme Court of Canada. Dr. Hamalengwa specialized as well in human rights advocacy before the Human a Rights Tribunal of Ontario and in Immigration and Deportation Law before the Federal Court and Federal Court of Appeal. In criminal courts, he specialized in trial advocacy defending a number of significant murder cases. He developed the strategy of Class Action Law Suits against systemic racial profiling and filed class action law suits against both the Federal and Provincial governments and police boards and police services.

Dr. Hamalengwa has also battled his own cases in courts and the Law Society of Upper Canada on racial profiling and to advance the principle of the equal application and benefit of the law without discrimination on any specified or analogous grounds.

Before leaving Canada for Zambia in 2016, Dr. Hamalengwa was an active member of the Toronto community, founding or co-founding many organizations like Forum For African Students in Toronto (FAST)(1980); African Human Rights

Research Association (1983 in Strasbourg, France); York Student Movement Against Apartheid; Development And Underdevelopment Series; Nelson Mandela Law Society (1986); Lawyers Against Apartheid (1989); African Canadian Legal Clinic and others.

He has served as an Adjudicator on the Liquor Licence Board Of Ontario between 1991 and 1994 and the Board of Inquiry under the Human Rights Code between 1995 and 1998.

His passion for politics and activism made him run for Mayor of Toronto in 1997.

His many travels, conferences and written words reflect his advocacy for human rights issues in Canada and at a broader level in the International Law of human Rights fora. He writes and argues with much fervor and outspoken candidness heated themes about social justice, racial profiling, government corruption, appointment of minority and female judges to all courts including the Supreme Court of Canada and other social issues. He is a specialist in the area of diversity and human resources in the judicial and legal sector.

During the many intervening years, Dr. Hamalengwa has written a legal/ criminal

/immigration/political column, which appeared weekly or regularly in Pride newspaper (Toronto, ON., Canada) ; African Affairs (Montreal, QC, Canada), Contrast Newspaper (Toronto, On., Canada), Share newspaper and Diversity News(Toronto, ON., Canada).

His articles and letters have also appeared in various magazines and newspapers such as For the Defence , Law Times , Lawyers Weekly, Law Union News, Canadian Lawyer, Nairobi Law Monthly, The Platform and newspapers such as Globe and Mail , Toronto Star , National Post , The Zambia Daily Mail, The Post (Zambia), The Mast (Zambia), The African Executive, Pambazuka and many online forums like the Zambian Eye, and others.

He has published so far ten major books and others are still in progress.

He worked in Washington, DC for a human rights organization and has traveled to Australia, Brazil, Kenya, Namibia, Japan, China, Europe, Hong Kong, Nigeria, Cuba, South Africa, Tanzania, Grand Cayman Islands, Jamaica, Zimbabwe, Egypt and other parts of the world on human rights causes and the reform of criminal law or to study law and tourism.

Dr. Hamalengwa picks his heroes carefully: for many years he worshipped heroes like Nelson Mandela, Muhammad Ali, Thurgood Marshall, Paul Robeson, Mahatma Gandhi, Johnnie Cochran and other legal giants and social justice advocates.

His passion and admiration for Nelson Mandela led him to form the Nelson Mandela Law Society in 1986 at Osgoode Hall Law School, named after his hero. He also championed the idea of bestowing an award of recognition to Nelson Mandela resulting in the award of the Honorary Doctorate of Laws to Nelson Mandela by York University, Toronto, Canada on 16 June 1989 (this was the first Canadian University to do so) and later the formation of Nelson Mandela Academy of Applied Legal Studies in 1996, an institution that reflects his passion for legal education and legal advocacy. This school trained paralegals for self-employment, a much needed service in the visible minority community in Toronto in order to take legal education to people at the grass-roots level for self employment and empowerment. Education is a never ending investment in oneself.

Dr. Hamalengwa also marked his presence in the Toronto Community by sponsoring many African events among a few are the African Canadian Achievement Awards where for many years he sponsored the law award which recognizes the contributions of lawyers, judges and organizations to the better administration of justice in the community and MissAfriCanada Pageant 2004 which aimed at training young women especially for self awareness, confidence in self and self assertiveness. Dr. Hamalengwa has received many awards for his service to the community and for his efforts in the education sector.

Dr. Munyonzwe Hamalengwa is in 2017, serving as the Dean of the School of Law at Zambian Open University, Lusaka, Zambia.

OTHER BOOKS BY THIS AUTHOR

Hamalengwa M. (2017). The Book On Judges. Diamond Books. Toronto, Canada

Hamalengwa M. (Ed). (2017). Political Halley's Comet: The Death Penalty In Global Comparative Perspective. Diamond Books. Toronto, Canada

Hamalengwa M. (2017). African-Canadians Under Legal, Judicial, Political and Media Attack. Africa In Canada Press. Toronto, Canada.

Hamalengwa M. (Ed) (2016). The Case Against Tribalism in Zambia. Africa In Canada Press. Toronto, Canada.

Hamalengwa M. (2015). Getting Away with Impunity: International Criminal Law and The Prosecution Of Apartheid Criminals. Africa in Canada Press. Toronto, Canada.

Hamalengwa M. (2012). The Politics of Judicial Diversity and Transformation: Canada; USA; UK, Australia; South Africa; Israel; Colonial and post-colonial world and international tribunals. Africa in Canada Press. Toronto, Canada.

Hamalengwa, M (2002) How Are We Gonna Win This One: Doing Time WITH Clay C. Ruby, Criminal Lawyer Extraordinaire. Africa in Canada Press, Toronto.

Hamalengwa M. (1992). Class Struggles In Zambia, 1889-1989 & The Fall of Kenneth Kaunda 1990-1991. University Press of America. New York, USA.

Hamalengwa, M (1991) Thoughts Are Free: Prison Experience and Reflections on Law and Politics in General. Africa in Canada Press, Toronto

Hamalengwa M, Flinterman C and Dankwa EVO (eds). (1988). The International Law Of Human Rights in Africa. Martinus Nijhoff Publishers. Dordrecht. Holland.

LIST OF CHAPTERS IN BOOKS

Hamalengwa M. (2015). Foreword. Public Intellectualism. In Mwenda K. (2015). Public Intellectualism through Metaphors and Musings. Africa in Canada Press. Toronto. Canada.

Hamalengwa M. (1992). The Legal System of Zambia: Law, Politics And Development in Historical Perspective. In E Bondzi-Simpson (ed). The law and Economic Development in The Third World. Praeger. New York, USA. First Chapter.

Hamalengwa M. (1991). The Legal System of Zambia. In W Krawiet. (ed). Legal Theories. Verlag Duncker, Germany. First Chapter

Hamalengwa M. (1985). Primitive Accumulation and the Reproduction Of Rural Population In Africa. In J Havet. The Village and Shantytown, Retention and Migration Of Rural Populations Of Africa. University of Ottawa Publications. Ottawa, Canada. First Chapter.

Hamalengwa M. (1984). The Contradictions of Post-Colonial Social Transformation: Mozambique, Angola and Zimbabwe. In D Wilson. Africa: A Continent in Crisis. Ontario Institute in

Studies in Education Press. Toronto, Canada.

Hamalengwa M. (1984). Class and Nation: A Contribution to The Debate on the Politics of Liberation in South Africa. In D Wilson. Africa: a continent in crisis. Ontario Institute in Studies in Education Press. Toronto, Canada.

JOURNAL ARTICLES

Hamalengwa M. (2016) Memorandum on Class Action Law Suits Based on Racial Profiling in Ontario, Canada in ZAOU L. J, forthcoming.

Hamalengwa M. (2016). Don't Talk about Diversification. Just Do It. Zambia's bulletin and record. June 2016.

Hamalengwa M. (2015). The Case for The Establishment of an International Tribunal Against Apartheid in African Executive, Nairobi, Kenya, June 2015.

Hamalengwa M. (1992). The Death Penalty in the Context of the Crime of Apartheid. Social Justice. 18: 95-105.

Hamalengwa M. (1986). Human Rights and Development in Geneva-Africa, September 1986

Hamalengwa M and cobbah J. 1986). The Human Rights Literature of Africa. Human Rights Quarterly. February

Hamalengwa M. (1985). The Political Economy of Human Rights in Africa. Journal of African Marxists. 7.

Hamalengwa M. (1983). The political economy of human rights in Africa: historical and contemporary perspectives. Philosophy and social action. IX (3) 15-26.

CONFERENCE PROCEEDINGS

Hamalengwa M. (2003). The role of the judiciary in racial profiling: the case of Canada. In Proceedings of the 18th International Conference of the International Society for the Reform of the Criminal Law, Convergence of Criminal Justice and Building Bridges. The Hague, Netherlands, 23-28 August, 2003.

Hamalengwa M. (2003). Problems and prospects in the prosecution and defence of international terrorists. In Proceedings of the 18th international Conference of the International Society for the Reform of the Criminal Law, Convergence of Criminal Justice and Building Bridges. The Hague, Netherlands, 23-28 August, 2003.

Hamalengwa M. (2003). Revolution and counter - revolution: problems of litigating race in criminal and immigration cases in Canada, an exploratory analysis of judicial resistance to allegations of racial profiling. In Proceedings of the 2nd Annual Human Rights Symposium, Focus on Racial Discrimination. Toronto, Canada, 22-23 May 2003.

Hamalengwa M. (2000). Constitutional challenges to the differential treatment of Canadian and non-

Canadian citizens. In Proceedings of the International Conference of the International Society for the Reform of the Criminal Law, Human Rights and Administration of Criminal Justice. Johannesburg, South Africa, 3-7 December, 2000.

Hamalengwa M. (1994). Problems with the proceeds of crime legislation under Canada's criminal law. In Proceedings of the International Conference of the International Society for the Reform of the Criminal Law, Proceeds of Crime. Hong Kong, China, December 1994.

Hamalengwa M. (1994). African-Canadians under legal, judicial, political and media attack. In Proceedings of the Ad Hoc Group of Africans Canadians Conference on African-Canadians Under Legal, Judicial, Political and Legal Attack. Toronto, Canada. 24 September, 1994.

Hamalengwa M. (1989). A contribution to the debate on civilian control of police powers in Toronto 1980 to 1989. In Proceedings of the International Conference of the International Society for the Reform of the Criminal Law. Sydney, Australia, March 1989.

Hamalengwa M. (1987). The application of the amended Canadian Criminal Code to Apartheid

Criminals in Canada. In Proceedings of the Conference, Political Halle 's Comet: Law, Politics and the Death Penalty in Global Comparative Perspective organized by the Nelson Mandela Law Society of Osgoode Hall Law School, Toronto, Canada. 20-21 October, 1987.

BOOK REVIEWS

Hamalengwa M. (2015). Police state in our times. Review of Spence G's Police State: How America's Cops Get Away With Murder. St. Martin's Press, New York, USA, 2015. African Executive, Nairobi, Kenya, September 2015.

Hamalengwa M. (2000). Justice delayed: Cassius Clay versus the USA. Review of Bingham H and Wallace M. Muhammad Ali's Greatest Fight: Cassius Clay V. The United States of America. Evans and Company, New York, USA. Law Times. Toronto, Canada. September 2000.

Hamalengwa M. (1990). Young offenders new law in Canada. Review of Platt P. (1989). Young offenders law in Canada. Butterworths. Toronto, Canada. Criminal Law Quarterly. 32:394.

Hamalengwa M. (1990). Native survival in Australia. Review of Martin P. (ed). (1988). Raparapa: stories from the fitzroy river drovers. Magabala Books, Broome, Australia. Canadian Native Law Reporter. 4:1-2.

Hamalengwa M. (1990). A new kid on the block. Review of Watt D and Fuerst M. (1990). 1990 Tremeesr's Criminal Code. Criminal Lawyers ' Association Newsletter. 1:36-37.

Hamalengwa M. (1989). The dialectics of las and politics. Review of Mandel M. (1989). The charter of rights and the legalization of politics in Canada. Wall and Thompson, Toronto, Canada. Obiter dicta. 3 April 1989.

Hamalengwa M. (1989). Order without law: review of books on South Africa. Obiter dicta. 27 February 1989.

Hamalengwa M. (1989). Feminism: The New Frontier. Review of Adamson N, Briskin L and Mcphail M. (1988). Feminist Organizing for Changes: the contemporary women's movement in Canada. Oxford, Toronto, Canada and Day S and Persky S. (1988). The Supreme Court of Canada decision on abortion. New Star Books, Vancouver, Canada. Obiter dicta. 13 February 1989.

Hamalengwa M. (1983). The CIA in South East Asia. Review of McGehee R. (1983). Deadly deceits: my 25 years in the CIA. Sheridan, New York, USA. Crime and Social Justice. No. 20, 1983.

Hamalengwa M. (1982). The struggle continues. Review of Petras J. (1981). Class, state and power in the third world. Allanheld and Osman, Montclair, USA. Human Rights Internet Reporter. 7 (5), 1982.

RESEARCH REPORTS

Hamalengwa M. (2016). A proposal for the Establishment of the graduate studies programme in the School of Law at Zambian Open University. Submitted to the Dean of the School of Law, Zambian Open University. Lusaka, Zambia, May 2016.

Hamalengwa M. and Mwewa C. (2014). Critical notes on the legal system of Zambia. A submission made to the Legal and Justice Sector Reform Commission of Zambia. Lusaka, Zambia. September 2014.

Hamalengwa M. and Mwewa C. (2012). A proposal towards the establishment of the Michael Mundale School of Business Establishment and Legal studies. Toronto, Canada, 2012.

Hamalengwa M. (2010). The politics of war crimes legislation in Canada. York Research Series. Toronto. Canada. February 2010.

Hamalengwa M. (2000). Practising law in the public interest. Submission made to Supreme Court of Canada Justice Peter Cory's Commission entitled, A Framework for Regulating Paralegal

Practice in Ontario. Toronto, Canada, February 2000.

Hamalengwa M. (1998). Reducing derivative costs to Ontario's Criminal Justice Process and other related issues. Submission to the Criminal Justice Review Committee of Ontario. Toronto, Canada. April 1998.

Hamalengwa M. (1996). Professional underdevelopment and systematic discrimination: prospects for professional development for minority lawyers in Canada". Submission to the Canadian Bar Association's Task Force on Racial Equality in the Legal Profession, chaired by Professor Joanne St. Lewis. Toronto, Canada, 16 December 1996.

Hamalengwa M. (1993). Has the Canadian Charter of Rights and Freedoms demobilized Canada's democracy? A thesis submitted to Professors Ian Green, George Szablowski and Reg Whitaker. Toronto, Canada.

Hamalengwa M. (1992). The law and politics of abortion in Canada. A report submitted on behalf of the coalition for pro-choice politics. Toronto, Canada.

Hamalengwa M. (1990). War crimes and Canadian immigration law and policy. Submission

Presented to Marlys Edwardh, Barrister and Solicitor. Toronto, Canada.

Hamalengwa M. (1990). Information, freedom and censorship: the case of Canada. Report on the freedom of information in Canada submitted to "Article 19" Group. London, England.

Hamalengwa M. (1990). Does Canada's new amendments to its Criminal Code apply to Apartheid Criminals. Submission made to the Commission of Inquiry into Apartheid on Parliament Hill. Ottawa, Canada, 25 May 1990.

Hamalengwa M. (1989). Judicial power and discretion in criminal law: how judges protect and defend their inherent power under the Canadian Charter of Rights and Freedoms. Submitted to Clayton Ruby for "The Charter and Sentencing Commission". Ottawa, Canada.

Hamalengwa M. (1989). Retroactive legislation and political offence exception to extradition and deportation. Consultative Research Report submitted to Marlys Edwardh, Barrister and Solicitor. Toronto, Canada.

Hamalengwa M. (1989). What constitutes an act that is contrary to the purposes and principles of the United Nations. Consultative Research Report on the Acts Contrary to the Purposes and

Principles of the United Nations. Ruby and Edwardh, Barristers and Solicitors. Toronto, Canada.

Hamalengwa M. (1989). Political offences and extradition in international law. Consultative Report submitted to Marlys Edwardh, Barrister and Solicitor, on Extradition in International Law. Toronto, Canada.

Hamalengwa M. (1986). Report on race and ethnic relations at York University. Being a member of the Presidential Committee on Race and Ethnic Relations at York University, Chair Professor Cumming P. Toronto, Canada. 1986.

Hamalengwa M. (1984). The politics of international education with respect to foreign students at York University. A Report Commissioned by the Canadian Union of Educational Workers, Local 3. Toronto, Canada. 1984. Pp.140

FEEDBACK

Now that you have read the book ...

Was it interesting?

Did you enjoy what you wanted to read?
Was there any room for improvement?

Let us know at:

http://www.hamalengwa.ca/feedback

Your feedback is highly appreciated.
Thank you!

MY AUTOBIOGRAPHY

THOUGHTS ARE FREE

PRISON EXPERIENCE AND REFLECTIONS ON LAW AND POLITICS IN GENERAL

THE INTERNATIONAL LAW OF
HUMAN RIGHTS
IN AFRICA
BASIC DOCUMENTS AND
ANNOTATED BIBLIOGRAPHY
DR. MUNYONZWE HAMALENGWA
PhD (Law).

POLITICAL HALLEY'S COMET

THE DEATH PENALTY IN GLOBAL COMPARATIVE PERSPECTIVES

CASE STUDIES OF
Canada, India, Apartheid South Africa, Nigeria, Jamaica, Grenada, Uganda Nazi War Crimes and International Law

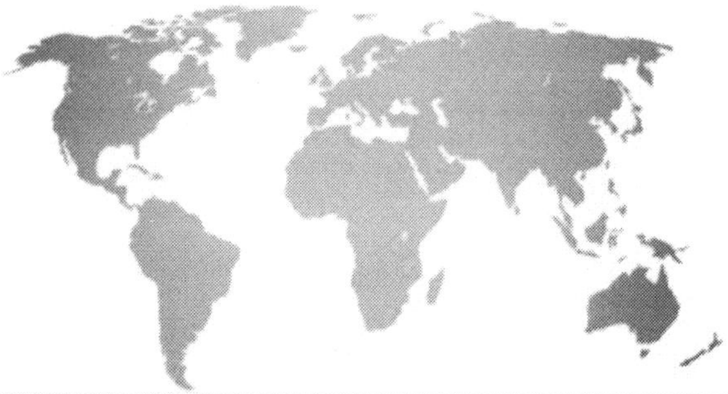

DR. MUNYONZWE HAMALENGWA
PhD (Law).

THE POLITICS

OF JUDICIAL DIVERSITY AND TRANSFORMATION

DR. MUNYONZWE HAMALENGWA
PhD (Law).

GETTING AWAY WITH IMPUNITY

INTERNATIONAL CRIMINAL LAW AND SOUTH AFRICAN APARTHEID CRIMINALS

DR. MUNYONZWE HAMALENGWA

PhD (Law).

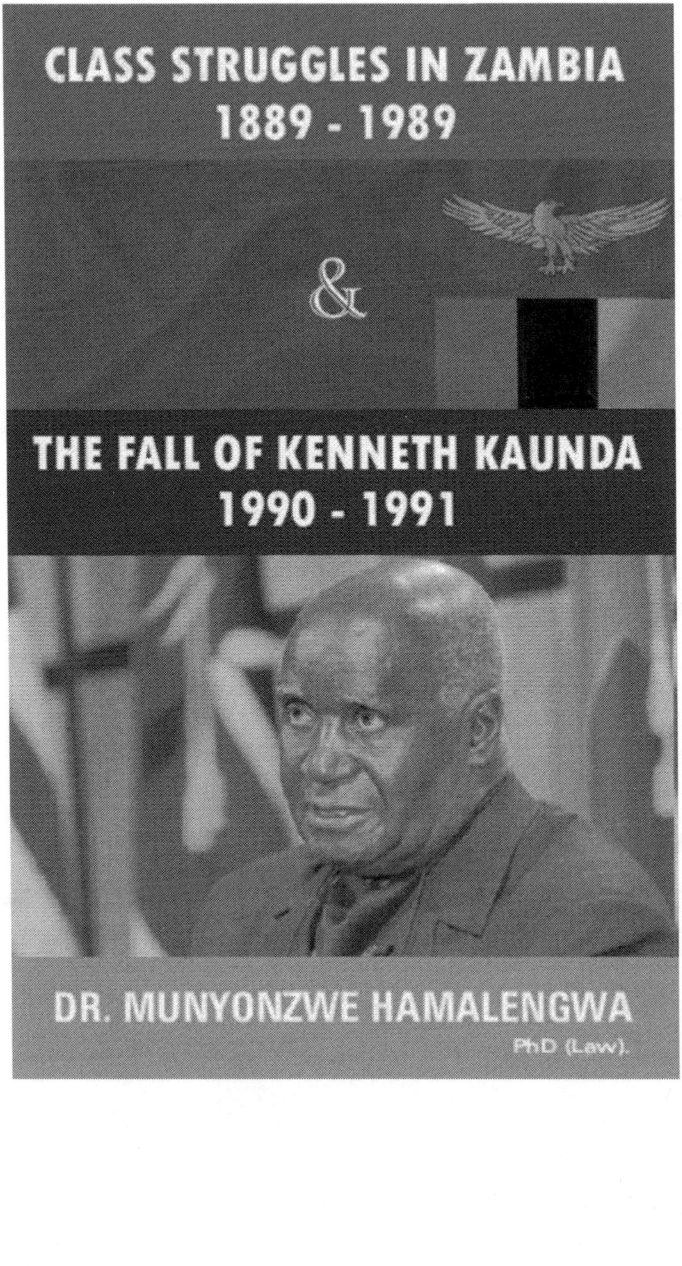
CLASS STRUGGLES IN ZAMBIA
1889 - 1989
&
THE FALL OF KENNETH KAUNDA
1990 - 1991
DR. MUNYONZWE HAMALENGWA
PhD (Law).

TRIBAL POLITICS A TIME BOMB IN ZAMBIA

THE CASE AGAINST TRIBALISM IN ZAMBIA

COMPILED BY

DR. MUNYONZWE HAMALENGWA

PhD (Law).

FROM THE DIARY OF AN ARTICLING STUDENT

HOW

ARE WE GONNA WIN THIS ONE

VOLUME 1

DOING TIME FOR **CLAYTON C. RUBY**

CRIMINAL LAWYER EXTRAORDINAIRE

DR. MUNYONZWE HAMALENGWA

PhD (Law).

AFRICAN CANADIANS

UNDER

LEGAL, JUDICIAL, POLITICAL, POLICE, AND MEDIA

ATTACK

STRATEGIES FOR SURVIVAL

DR. MUNYONZWE HAMALENGWA

PhD (Law).

NOTES

NOTES

Made in the USA
Monee, IL
08 November 2026

68063221R00203